10

MINUTE GUIDE TO

LOTUS NOTES MAIL 4.6

by Jane Calabria
and Dorothy Burke

A Division of Macmillan Computer Publishing
201 West 103rd St., Indianapolis, Indiana 46290 USA

We dedicate this book to Al Valvano and his family.

©1998 by Que® Corporation

International Standard Book Number: 0-7897-1534-1
Library of Congress Catalog Card Number: 97-80539

99 98   8 7 6 5 4 3

Interpretation of the printing code: The rightmost double-digit number is the year of the book's first printing; the rightmost single-digit number is the number of the book's printing. For example, a printing code of 98-1 shows that this copy of the book was printed during the first printing of the book in 1998.

Printed in the United States of America

Publisher David Dwyer

Executive Editor Al Valvano

Acquisitions Editor Stephanie Layton

Development Editor Jim Chalex

Brand Marketing Director Alan Bower

Editorial Services Director Carla Hall

Managing Editor Sarah Kearns

Production Editor Tom Lamoureux

Copy Editor Juliet MacLean

Technical Editor Debbie Lynd

Book Designer Kim Scott

Cover Designer Dan Armstrong

Indexer Joy D. Lee

Production Team Erin Danielson, Jennifer Earhart, DiMonique Ford, Laura A. Knox, Heather Stephenson

CONTENTS

INTRODUCTION

Lotus Notes is considered by many to be *the* groupware product of the 90s. Ever evolving to meet the collaboration, communication, and Internet needs of businesses, Release 4.6 of Lotus Notes focuses on the Notes client. New features of 4.6 include improved navigation features (Portfolios), Web Navigator integration with Internet Explorer, and contact management capabilities within the Personal Name and Address Book. These features and more are introduced in *the Ten Minute Guide to Lotus Notes Mail 4.6.*

WELCOME TO THE 10 MINUTE GUIDE TO LOTUS NOTES MAIL 4.6

This book focuses on the basics of Lotus Notes Mail, introduces general email concepts and the Basics of Lotus Notes Mail, and teaches you the advanced features of Mail. You can work through the book lesson by lesson, building upon your skills, or you can use the book as a quick reference when you want to perform a new task. Features and concepts are presented in lessons that take 10 minutes or less to complete.

If you are new to Notes, start at the beginning of the book. If you've used Notes before, you might want to skip the first few lessons and work from there. Use the Table of Contents and select the lessons that cover features of the program you haven't yet used. If you travel with Lotus Notes Mail on your laptop, the compact size of this book is perfect for fitting into your laptop or notebook case.

WHO SHOULD USE THIS BOOK

The *10 Minute Guide to Lotus Notes Mail 4.6* is for anyone who:

- Has Lotus Notes or Notes Mail installed on his PC or laptop

- Needs to learn Notes Mail quickly
- Wants to explore some of the new Mail features of Release 4.6
- Needs a task-based Lotus Notes Mail tutorial
- Requires a compact Notes Mail reference guide

CONVENTIONS USED IN THIS BOOK

To help you move through the lessons easily, **On-screen text**, **What you type**, and **Items you select** (Commands, options, and icons you select or keys you press) appear in bold type.

In telling you to choose menu commands, this book uses the format *menu title*, *menu command*. For example, the statement "choose **File**, **Properties**" means "open the File menu and select the Properties command."

In addition to these conventions, the *10 Minute Guide to Lotus Notes Mail 4.6* uses the following icons to identify helpful information:

- **Plain English**   New or unfamiliar terms are defined in "plain English."

- **Timesaver Tips**   Look here for ideas that help you cut corners and avoid confusion.

- **Panic Button**   This icon identifies areas in which new users often run into trouble, offering practical solutions to those problems.

ACKNOWLEDGMENTS

A lot of hard work went into completing this project, and we'd like to thank all of those involved. First and foremost, our gratitude goes to Macmillan Computer Publishing for becoming the leader in Lotus Notes books. Their commitment to providing quality Lotus Notes books in a timely fashion to the Notes community makes this a very exciting time to be writing and working with their dedicated staff. Thanks, too, to our new Notes team at Macmillan: Al Valvano, Executive Editor; Stephanie Layton, Acquisitions Editor; Jim Chalex and Ami Frank, Development Editors. Thanks to our production team, Tom Lamoureux and Juliet MacLean.

From Here...

For more information on Lotus Notes, try these other Macmillan Computer Publishing books:

- *The 10 Minute Guide to Lotus Notes 4.6*   Use discussion databases, understand workflow, and learn the features of Notes beyond its email capabilities.

- *Special Edition Using Lotus Notes and Domino 4.6*   The ultimate Lotus Notes companion for the advanced user.

- *Teach Yourself Lotus Notes 4.6 in 24 Hours*   The perfect book for those new to Notes.

To learn about all of the MCP Lotus Notes books, visit their web site at **www.mcp.com**.

For Lotus Notes press releases, technical information, and new product information, visit the Lotus web sites. The following Lotus sites contain information relevant to the Notes client:

- **www.lotus.com**   The Lotus home page, where you can find information on all Lotus products and services, including support and access to other Lotus Notes sites.

- **www2.lotus.com/education.nsf**   The Lotus Education site, where you can find course descriptions, schedules, locations, certification information, and Lotus Authorized Education Centers for Lotus Notes and other Lotus Products.

- **www2.lotus.com/learningcenters**   To learn about Notes features, take a Notes guided tour.

To access information on the web, you need a web browser and Internet connection. See your Notes administrator if you need information on connecting your Notes workstation to the web.

TRADEMARKS

All terms mentioned in this book that are known to be trademarks have been appropriately capitalized. Que cannot attest to the accuracy of this information. Use of a term in this book should not be regarded as affecting the validity of any trademark or service mark.

UNDERSTANDING LOTUS NOTES CONCEPTS

In this lesson, you learn about Lotus Notes concepts and how Lotus Notes stores information. You also learn how Lotus Notes presents that stored information to you.

UNDERSTANDING CLIENTS AND SERVERS

Lotus Notes is based on client/server technology. Your PC is the Lotus Notes client, requesting and receiving information from the Domino server. In the office, you're "attached" to the server over your network. At home, you can "attach" to the server through a phone line or dial-up connection. On the road, with a laptop, you can store the information you need from the server on your C: drive or "locally."

You communicate with the Notes server, officially called the "Domino" server, through a series of wires and cables (hardware) and networking software. The information you request is stored in Lotus Notes applications, or databases. The Domino server usually stores those databases so that many "clients" can access them at one time. In most cases, when you double-click a Lotus Notes icon, you are actually opening a database stored on the server. Your client (your PC) requests that database from the server and when the database opens, the database that resides on the server appears on your PC's screen (see Figure 1.1).

Figure 1.1 is similar to the connection you have at work to your file server. Often, you store work that you have created in other software programs (other than Lotus Notes) on the file server on your network at the office. For example, you might create a Lotus 1-2-3 spreadsheet or a Word document. When you save these files, you might save them on your drive F:, which is actually space dedicated to you for storage on the file server.

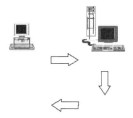

FIGURE 1.1   How clients and servers work.

Three types of Lotus Notes clients include Lotus Notes Mail: Lotus Notes Designer, Notes Client, and Notes Mail.

UNDERSTANDING DATABASES

There are many different uses for Notes databases. One database might hold customer information, whereas another might hold information about company projects, and still another might hold your mail. Even your email is a Lotus Notes database. Databases are like miniprograms or applications. Just as you might have multiple spreadsheet files with different formulas and calculations for solving various business problems, Notes databases are usually created to handle a specific business process, such as customer service calls, client tracking for sales, or expense reporting.

Although many Notes databases are created by Application Developers, the mail database is created automatically by Notes and comes with all three types of Lotus Notes clients previously mentioned. If you have Notes Mail installed, you can use only the Lotus Notes Mail database. If you use Notes Designer or Notes Client, however, you have a larger software program that includes more features than Notes Mail; with the Notes Client, you can use database applications that are created by Application Developers, and with the Notes Designer, you can be the Application Developer.

The mail database is different from other Lotus Notes databases you might be using because it is a private database for your use only. Others cannot access or use your mail database without your permission. On the other hand, other databases are designed for use by the entire company or departments within the company.

Even though your mail database is private, it is stored on the Domino 4.6 server. While you are at work and connected to the network, your mail icon usually acts as a pointer: When you open your mail database, you are actually opening the copy that resides on the Domino server. Remote or mobile users usually have a special type of copy—called a replica copy—of the database that resides on their laptop, on their desktop computer at home, or in a remote office, enabling them to read and create mail while disconnected from the Domino server.

UNDERSTANDING DOCUMENTS AND FORMS

Lotus Notes databases store everything in documents. Each document that represents data you have entered contains fields for the pieces of that data. It's a little weird to say that you never really see these documents, but you don't. If you are familiar with other database systems, consider documents as being like records: A record contains fields. In this sense, Lotus Notes works like other kinds of databases. What's different about Lotus Notes is that you don't actually see the records, or documents. You see the contents of the documents by looking at them through forms.

 Database Record   A collection of data entered into fields. For example, consider the phone book. When you look for a person in the phone book, you look for information pertaining to a specific individual. That information is the name, address, and phone number, which would be considered *fields*. All of the information for that individual is a *record*, and all of the records in the phone book combined are the database.

Every database in Lotus Notes has custom forms designed for creating, displaying, and printing documents within that database. The Lotus Notes Mail database is no exception. In the Mail database, there are many forms. The ones you'll use the most are the Memo, Reply, Calendar Entry, and Task forms. These forms contain fields such as the To field and the Subject field. It's not important to memorize all the fields and forms, but it is good to understand that you work in fields and forms (see Figure 1.2).

Fields   Form

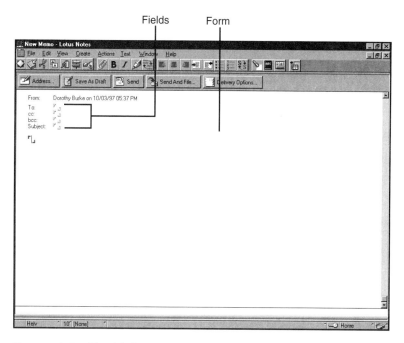

FIGURE 1.2   The Mail Memo form.

UNDERSTANDING VIEWS

Fields of information stored in records (documents) that you see through forms are accessed by looking at a view. A view contains a list of documents and displays the contents of specified fields in those documents; it acts like a table of contents for the documents in the database. The Inbox view of mail is nothing more than a listing of the documents (mail) you've received with the contents of the From field, the date the document was delivered, and the Subject field displayed (see Figure 1.3). When you want to read your mail, double-click the piece of mail in the view to read your mail document through a form (the mail memo form).

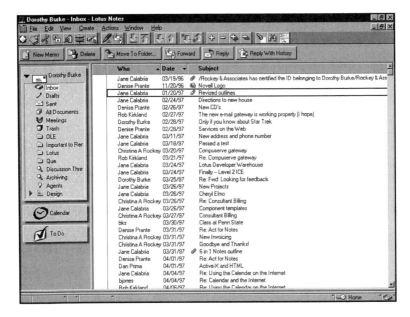

FIGURE 1.3   The Inbox View listing documents.

In this lesson, you learned about clients and servers. You also learned about Lotus Notes databases and how Lotus Notes displays the contents of its databases. In the next lesson, you will learn more specifics about the mail database.

GETTING STARTED WITH LOTUS NOTES

2

In this lesson, you learn how to move around the Lotus Notes workspace. You also learn how customize workspace page tabs.

USING THE WORKSPACE

To start Lotus Notes and access the workspace, click the **Start** button on the Taskbar and select **Lotus Notes** from the Programs, Lotus Applications submenu. The Notes workspace appears, similar to the one shown in Figure 2.1.

In the Notes workspace, you should see your Lotus Notes Mail database icon and icons for your Public and Personal Address Books, the Favorites database, the Journal, and possibly, other databases that your company uses.

The Lotus Notes workspace looks similar to and acts much like other programs you use in Windows:

- The *title bar* shows the current location and the program name. The information in the title bar changes to display information about a particular database when it is opened.

- The *menu bar* has all of the menu selections for the current window, so the menu bar changes, depending on the Notes window that is active. When you click a menu name, a submenu displays all the commands associated with that menu item. As in Windows, if a command is dimmed or gray, it is not currently available.

Title bar   Menu bar
    Mail database   Toolbar with Tabbed workspace
                SmartIcons pages

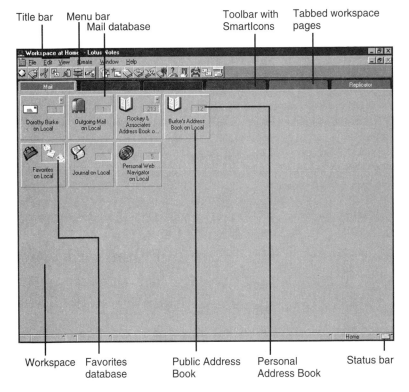

Workspace Favorites   Public Address Personal   Status bar
      database   Book   Address Book

FIGURE 2.1 The Lotus Notes workspace.

- The *toolbar* contains icons you can use in lieu of using the menu; Lotus calls these icons *SmartIcons* (more about these icons later in the lesson).

- The *workspace* has several tabbed pages to help you organize your work. You can put different database icons on different pages (you'll learn how to do this later in this lesson). To move from one tabbed page to another, simply click the tab of the page you want to see. The page moves to the front and becomes the "active" workspace page.

- The *status bar* appears at the bottom of the screen. It contains information such as your location (in Figure 2.1, this is home) and gives you access to your mail, which you'll learn more about in Lesson 4. The status bar also changes, based on the Notes window that is active.

TIP   **Shortcut Keys**   You can quickly access commands in the menu bar by pressing the **Alt** key and the underlined letter of the menu or command name. For example, pressing **Alt+F** has the same effect as clicking the word **File** with your mouse.

CUSTOMIZING WORKSPACE PAGES

One of the first things you might want to do when planning the organization of your workspace is to give names to your workspace pages. There are probably eight workspace pages on your workspace right now. You can put names on the tabs, select the colors for the tabs, and add new tabbed pages whenever you need more. To further organize your information, you also can move database icons from one workspace page to another.

NAMING TABS AND CHANGING TAB COLORS

To name a tab or change its color, follow these steps:

1. With your right mouse button, click the tab or the open gray area of the current workspace page (see Figure 2.2).

Right-click here

FIGURE 2.2   Workspace tab of the current page.

2. A pop-up menu appears. Select **Workspace Properties**.

3. The Properties box appears, as shown in Figure 2.3. In the **Workspace Page Name** text box, type the name you want to give the tab. For this example, type **Mail**. (Reserve this page strictly for your Mail database, your Favorites database, and your Address Book databases during the rest of the lessons in this book.)

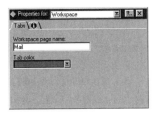

FIGURE 2.3 The Properties box.

4. To change the color of the tab, click the **Tab Color** drop-down menu. Click a color you like.

5. To close the Properties box and save your changes, click the Close (**X**) button in the upper-right corner of the Properties box. You can now see your newly named tab.

Even though you have changed the color of a tab, the page itself does not change color. The page that is active, or in front, is always gray; instead, the tab colors help differentiate among pages.

TIP   **Naming Tabs** A quick way to make the Properties box appear is to double-click the tab you want to name. Then you can enter the name, select a color, and close the Properties box.

If you have other databases and want to organize them into separate workspace pages, simply name the tabs on your other workspace pages in preparation for moving your database icons to those pages (you'll learn how to move database icons in the next section).

Moving a Database Icon to a Different Workspace Page

If you have no other database icons on your workspace, you can experiment with moving database icons by using your Mail icon. If you move your Mail icon, however, be sure to move it back to the original workspace page. To move a database icon, follow these steps:

1. Click the database icon once to select it.

2. Drag the icon to the tab of the new workspace page where you want this icon to appear.

3. When a rectangle appears around the tab name of the new workspace page, release the mouse button.

4. Your icon should no longer appear on your current workspace page.

5. Click the new workspace page tab, and you will see your database icon.

Adding Tabs to the Workspace

Although your icons might not fill every page, you can use up all the tabs with different categories. You can add pages to your workspace and new pages that you add will appear to the left of the currently selected page. When you need an additional page or tab, follow these steps to create one:

1. Select **Create**, **Workspace Page** from the menu.

2. The new workspace tab is added to your workspace.

3. With your right mouse button, click the new workspace tab.

4. Select **Workspace Properties** from the pop-up menu.

5. Name the page and select a color for the tab in the Properties box.

6. Close the Properties box and save your changes.

CHANGING TO THE WORKSPACE BACKGROUND

The gray background of your workspace can be flat or textured. In this book, you see the flat workspace background in our illustrations because it prints more clearly. The textured background, however, gives your workspace a sense of depth.

To change your workspace background, do the following:

1. Choose **File**, **Tools**, **User Preferences** from the menu. The User Preferences dialog box appears (see Figure 2.4).

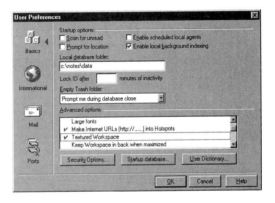

FIGURE 2.4   The User Preferences dialog box.

2. Under **Advanced Options**, click **Textured Workspace**. A check mark indicates that the option is turned on. If you click it when it's checked, the option turns off, and your workspace will be flat.

3. Click **OK**.

CHANGING THE INFORMATION DISPLAYED ON A DATABASE ICON

Database icons can provide information, such as the number of unread documents that are contained in the database (that is, documents that you have not read), the name of the database, and where you can find the database (on the Domino server or on your hard drive, "on local"). To select icon display information, consult the following:

- To display the number of unread documents, choose **View**, **Show Unread** from the menu.

- To display the location of the database, choose **View**, **Show Server Names**. If the database is on your server, your server name appears on the icon. If the database is on your hard drive (likely if you are a remote or mobile user),**On Local** appears on the icon as its location.

- To display the file name of the database, hold down the **Shift** key while selecting **View**, **Show Server Names**. This turns off the server name and displays the filename.

- To display both the location of the database and the filename, hold down the **b** key while selecting **View**, **Show Server Names**.

TURNING ON LARGE FONTS

Don't strain your eyes! If the text on the tabs of the worksheet and the database icons is difficult to read, there is a setting to make those fonts larger. This setting also affects the views and documents within the databases. It doesn't, however, change the size of all the type in the dialog boxes.

To change to larger fonts, follow these steps:

1. Choose **File**, **Tools**, **User Preferences** from the menu. The User Preferences dialog box appears (refer to Figure 2.4).

2. Under **Advanced Options**, select **Large Fonts** from the list. When you select this option, a check mark appears in front of it to indicate the option is turned on (clicking it again turns it off).

3. Click **OK**. The large fonts won't appear immediately, but you'll see them the next time you open Notes.

 I Can't Read the Title Bar!   Using large fonts can truncate information on the title bar. If you find that you can no longer see everything on the title bar, switch to a smaller font.

In this lesson, you learned about the standard elements of the Notes workspace and how to customize your workspace pages. In the next lesson, you'll learn about the SmartIcons and the Properties box.

Using the Properties Box and SmartIcons

In this lesson, you learn what the Properties box is and how to use it. You also learn how to use and customize the SmartIcons.

Using the Properties Box

Properties boxes present options that are related to menu commands. Similar to dialog boxes, they present the "properties" associated with an item you have selected. For example, the Properties box for a database indicates the database name, size, creation date, and other pertinent information. The Properties box *looks* like a dialog box, but it doesn't *act* quite the same. If you enter options in a dialog box, you must click OK or press Enter to accept your settings and apply them. Unlike changes you make in a dialog box, the changes you make in the Properties box are immediately applied. Also, you don't have to close the Properties box for the changes to take place.

Properties boxes are context sensitive—that is, depending on what you have selected or what task you're performing, the features in the Properties box change. When you're working with text, the Properties box shows text options. It shows workspace "properties" when you're working with the workspace. To know which options the Properties box is displaying, look at the title bar of the box (see Figure 3.1). The Properties For drop-down list box shows what feature the options modify. You can choose another feature from the drop-down list.

Title bar

Properties
SmartIcon

Close

Help

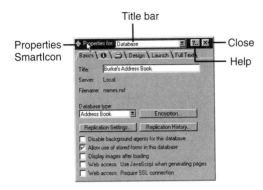

FIGURE 3.1 The Properties box, displaying database options.

TIP

Keep it Open! When you want to make several changes
to different objects on the same screen, you might want to
leave the Properties box open, instead of closing it each
time you finish your settings for a different item. If the box
gets in your way on the screen, point to the title bar of the
Properties box and drag the box to a new location. To
temporarily collapse the box, double-click the title bar—it
will show only the title bar and the tabs under it. Double-
click the title bar again to make the rest of the Properties
box reappear.

If you want some help with the options displayed on the Properties box, click the **Help** button (**?**).

There are several methods for opening the Properties box:

- Select an item, right-click it, and choose **Item Properties** from the pop-up menu. The item changes, depending on what you right-click. For example, if you
right-click a database icon, the choice on the pop-up
menu is **Database Properties**.

- Select an item, open the menu choice that relates to it, and choose **Item Properties**. For example, if you're working with text, you choose **Text** from the menu and then click **Text Properties**.

- ◇ Click the **Properties** SmartIcon button.

To close the Properties box, click **Close** (**X**).

USING SMARTICONS

SmartIcons (a Lotus term) are the icons located on the toolbar. Most of your Windows products contain a toolbar with icons that act as shortcuts or alternatives to using the menu. Some people find it faster to click a SmartIcon than to look through the menus to find choices such as opening a database or bolding text. The SmartIcons change as you work in different parts of Lotus Notes.

To help you understand the function of each SmartIcon, Lotus Notes has a feature that shows the SmartIcon's description. To see this brief description, hold your mouse over a SmartIcon. If the description does not appear, you might need to turn this feature on. Here's how to turn on the SmartIcon descriptions:

1. From your workspace, open the **File** menu and click **Tools** and then **SmartIcons**. The SmartIcons dialog box appears, as shown in Figure 3.2.

2. Under **Show**, select **Descriptions**.

3. Click **OK**.

To learn the purpose of each SmartIcon, place your cursor on the SmartIcon; a bubble appears, listing the description of the SmartIcon.

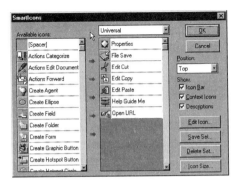

FIGURE 3.2   The SmartIcons dialog box.

You can change the default SmartIcon set (called the Universal
Set), by customizing it for your needs. For example, you might
find it convenient to have the Print icon on your toolbar. To add
or remove the Print icon:

1. From your workspace, open the **File** menu and choose
   Tools and **SmartIcons** from the menu.

2. The SmartIcon dialog box appears, as shown in Figure 3.3.
   The left panel shows available icons; the right panel
   shows icons that are currently selected for your "Universal Set" (the set in use). Scroll through the left panel of
   available icons until you locate the Printer icon.

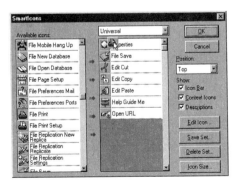

FIGURE 3.3   Customizing the SmartIcon set.

3. Drag the Printer icon from the left panel to the right panel. Position the icon on the right panel in the exact position you want it to appear on your toolbar. For example, placing this icon first on the list results in its appearing first (on the far left) on the toolbar.

4. Repositioning the Printer icon causes the icons to move down in the list so that your Printer icon is first on the list.

5. (**Optional**) To remove a SmartIcon from the toolbar, select it from the icons in the right panel and drag it to the left panel.

6. Click **OK** to save your changes and close the window. The Printer icon appears on the toolbar.

You also can change the size of your SmartIcons. To do so:

1. From your workspace, open the **File** menu; choose **Tools**, **SmartIcons** from the menu.

2. The SmartIcon dialog box appears (see Figure 3.4). Click the **Icon Size** button. The Icon Size dialog box appears (see Figure 3.4).

FIGURE 3.4   The Icon Size dialog box.

3. The default size for icons is small. Select large to change the icon size.

4. Click **OK** to close the Icon Size dialog box.

5. Click **OK** in the SmartIcon dialog box to save your changes and close the window.

You might want to change the position of your SmartIcon palette. The default position for your SmartIcon set is at the top of the screen. You can select Left, Right, Top, Bottom, or Floating.

 Floating Palette   When a floating palette is selected, the smarticon set appears in its own window rather than being anchored on the edge of the screen (as in Right, Left, Top, or Bottom). You can move the floating window around the screen by dragging its title bar; you can resize the window by dragging its borders.

To change the position of your SmartIcon set:

1. From your workspace, open the **File** menu, and click **Tools**, **SmartIcons** from the menu.

2. The SmartIcon dialog box appears (refer to Figure 3.3). Click the **Position** drop-down menu. Select the position you want for your SmartIcon set.

3. Click **OK** in the SmartIcon dialog box to save your changes and close the window.

The SmartIcon set now appears in its new position (see Figure 3.5).

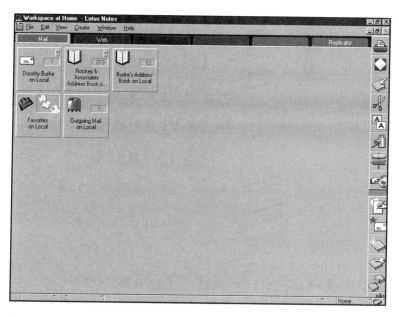

FIGURE 3.5   SmartIcon set with "Right" selected as position.

In this lesson, you learned about the Properties box and the SmartIcons and how to use them. In the next lesson, you learn about the mail database.

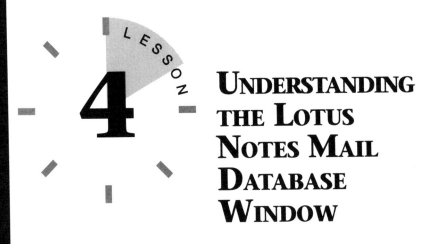

UNDERSTANDING THE LOTUS NOTES MAIL DATABASE WINDOW

In this lesson, you learn how to open your mail database, how to use views and folders, and how the Trash works.

OPENING THE MAIL DATABASE

Lotus Notes stores your mail in your mail database. The stored mail includes copies of messages you've received and sent, plus specialized documents such as calendar entries and tasks. Your Mail workspace page contains an icon that represents the mail database. This icon has a small picture of an envelope with your name on it. To open the database, double-click the mail database icon.

MOVING AROUND THE MAIL DATABASE WINDOW

The mail database window is divided into two panes (see Figure 4.1). On the left side, the Navigator pane displays the different views available in the database; each view has an icon associated with it along with text describing the contents of the view. Use the Navigator pane to select these different views.

Unread mail ⎯   View pane

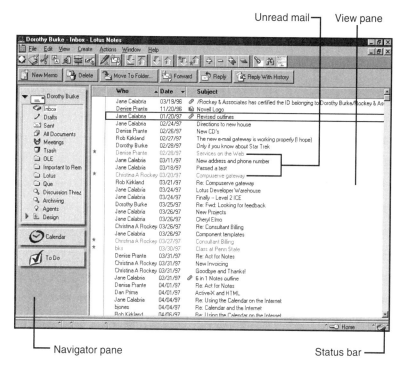

⎯ Navigator pane   Status bar ⎯

FIGURE 4.1   The mail database window.

As you select different view icons on the Navigator pane of your screen, the documents that appear on the right side of your screen (in the View pane) change. For example, if you select the Inbox icon on the left, the contents of your Inbox appear like a table of contents on the right. The Inbox view (on the right) shows you who sent the message, the date of the message, and a brief description of the contents. All the unread messages have a red star at the beginning of the line.

You can expand and collapse the mail icon by clicking the envelope in the Navigator pane. Figure 4.1 shows the mail view expanded.

No Messages?   If you're using Mail for the first time, you might not have any messages waiting. That will change quickly as you send mail messages to others and they reply back to you.

TIP   **Resizing the Panes**   You can change the size of the Navigator and View panes to see more of one side or the other. Point to the line separating the two panes until your mouse pointer turns into a two-headed arrow separated by a black line. Then, simply drag it to the left or right.

The status bar (located at the bottom of the screen— refer to Figure 4.1) indicates whether or not you're currently connected to your Domino server. A lightning bolt at the left of the status bar indicates that you are connected. No lightning bolt means that you are not currently connected to your server.

If you click the Mail icon on the right of the status bar, you see a pop-up menu (see Figure 4.2) that enables you to choose common mail tasks:

- Create Memo starts a new mail message.

- Scan Unread Mail provides a list of the mail you haven't read.

- Receive Mail retrieves new mail from the server.

- Send Outgoing Mail sends messages that you have written.

- Send & Receive Mail performs both actions at once.

- Open Mail opens the mail database.

FIGURE 4.2   The Mail pop-up menu.

To begin a task, select it from the pop-up menu. This pop-up menu is available in every window of Lotus Notes, so you can send and receive mail and perform other mail functions even when you're in another database or on the workspace itself.

You can find the Action bar (see Figure 4.3) at the top of the mail database window below the SmartIcons. The Action bar is context-sensitive and has several buttons on it. When you click one of the action buttons, it performs a program task such as saving your mail document.

FIGURE 4.3   The Action bar of the Inbox.

 Context-Sensitive   The available actions depend on your current task or context. For example, if you're reading a document, one of the available actions is to edit the document. Because you can't save a document you were just reading, the Save button does not appear. On the other hand, when you're editing a document, editing is no longer an available action, but saving the document is.

When you select the Inbox, there are six buttons on the Action bar:

- New Memo creates a new piece of mail.

- Delete marks a message for removal from the database.

- Move to Folder moves a document to a specific folder.

- Forward sends a copy of a message to someone who did not receive the original.

- Reply starts a new document that is a reply to a piece of mail.

- Reply with History sends a copy of the original message along with your reply.

You'll learn more about these buttons in Lesson 12.

USING FOLDERS AND VIEWS

The Navigator pane (refer to Figure 4.1) presents several folders and views for you to use when you work with your mail documents.

In Lesson 1, you learned that a view is a list of documents, similar to a table of contents of the database. In the mail database, a view lists your mail messages. There are different views that you can use to look at a list of mail messages sorted by date or by sender. Except for changing the way a view is sorted, you can't alter the contents of the view. You can create your own folders, however, and determine which messages you want to store in those folders. In Figure 4.1, OLE, Important to Remember, Lotus, and Que are all folders added by the user. In Lesson 13, you'll learn how to create folders.

As mentioned previously, the Navigator pane has a series of pre-manufactured views and folders. The Inbox is the default view when you open the mail database for the first time. From then on, the active view when you close your mail database is the view that appears the next time you open it.

Sometimes you write a message and decide not to send it right away. Maybe you need to add information to it or you're called away from your desk. You can save a message without sending it by storing it in the Drafts view. When you want to go back to the message and finish it, click the Drafts icon in the Navigator pane to see a list of your drafts. To finish your draft, select and open the document by double-clicking the document displayed in the view panel, finish your work, and send the message.

Mail displays the messages you sent in Sent unless you move or delete them. To check the messages you have already sent, click the Sent icon.

All Documents shows all the messages that are currently in your mail database.

Calendar displays a calendar with any entries you have made in the appropriate block for that day. From this view, you also can make appointments on your personal calendar and make appointments with others who use Notes Mail within your organization. You'll learn more about calendars in Lessons 19 and 20.

And what would the well-organized person be without a To Do list? You can use Lotus Notes Mail to assign tasks to other people, as well as to yourself. When you click the To Do icon, you see a list of these tasks. The View pane lists a description of each task, the due date, and the person assigned to do the task. You'll work extensively with tasks to populate your To Do list in Lesson 18.

Meetings is a list of your appointments sorted by date, time, and subject.

Documents that you mark for deletion are stored in Trash.

Use the Discussion Thread view to see messages grouped with their replies so you can follow an entire conversation.

The Archiving view lists the documents you archived from this database. You archive messages to save space in your mail database by creating a new database and sending your old and expired messages to that database. You'll learn to archive your old mail messages in Lesson 13.

Agents are like macros. They automate tasks such as managing documents, manipulating fields, and importing information from other applications. Although you use agents to complete tasks with your mail database, the creation of agents is usually done by an application developer.

Design enables you to change the design of Notes databases, including the views and forms. You might not even see this view, depending on the type of Notes client you are running. Changing the design of the mail database should not be done without the approval of your Notes administrator.

What Is a Default?   A predefined system setting that you can choose to override. For example, the default font for Lotus Notes Mail is Helvetica, but you can change it to another font.

All Documents View

When you have mail, you'll appreciate these different views. If you don't have any mail yet, don't panic. It's still a good exercise to click through these views. By the time you start receiving mail, you'll have a good grasp on how to move around the mail database.

Click the All Documents icon in the Navigator pane to see all of the documents in your mail database displayed in the View pane—both the ones you have sent and the ones you have received (see Figure 4.4). For each document, you can see who sent it, the date it was sent, and the subject of the message.

By default, the view is sorted by date in ascending order (oldest first). You can change the sort of the documents by the name of the person (who) in ascending order or by the date in descending order (newest first). However, you can't change the sort of all views. How can you tell whether or not you can sort a view? The column headers have little triangles on them. The Who column header has an up triangle that indicates that this column sorts in ascending order (alphabetically A to Z). The Date column has a down triangle, which means this column sorts in descending order (most recent to oldest).

To re-sort the columns, click the appropriate column header to change the order (you don't have to click right on the triangle). Clicking the Who column header sorts the documents alphabetically; clicking the Date column header sorts the documents in date order. You don't have the option to sort it both ways (by who, then by date) at the same time in this view. If the option to sort both ways were available in this view, the triangles would point both up and down on the column header. You might see that sort option in views for other databases.

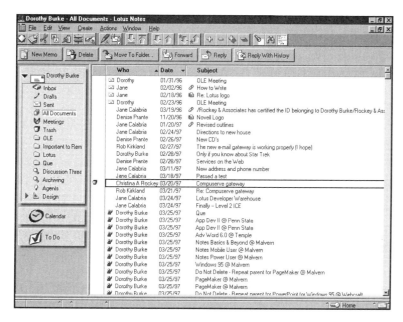

FIGURE 4.4   The All Documents view.

When connected to the Domino server at work, your mail might not appear in your view as quickly as it arrives in your mailbox. Lotus Notes can notify you with a beeping sound or with a message on the screen that says you have new mail.

To refresh your view and see the new mail listed, click the Refresh icon in the upper-left corner of the view pane or press F9. The refresh icon can appear in any view of Lotus Notes if a document has been added or modified during the time you have the view open. Use the F9 key to refresh a view when you see the refresh icon.

UNDERSTANDING TRASH

As you view your messages, you can mark the ones you don't want to keep by selecting the message and then clicking the Delete button in the Action bar or by pressing the Delete key on your keyboard. A Trash can icon appears in the document row. When you leave the database, Notes displays a message, asking if you want to delete the marked items. You can select Yes or No.

If you choose Yes, your messages are deleted from the database. If you choose No, your messages go into the Trash view, although you can still see them in the All Documents view (they'll have a Trash can icon in front of the document row). You can decide later if you want to keep them or not. You wouldn't be the first person to go through your trash to find something you shouldn't have thrown out.

When you click the Trash icon, you can select a document and pull it out of the Trash by clicking the Remove from Trash Action button. You can also empty your Trash, without being reminded. Emptying your Trash permanently removes all the documents listed there from the database, so be very sure you want to do this before you click the Empty Trash Action button.

In this lesson, you learned about opening your mail database, using the different views and folders, and how to use Trash. In the next lesson, you will learn about using Lotus Notes Help.

USING LOTUS NOTES HELP

In this lesson, you learn how to use Lotus Notes Help. You also learn how to perform searches within the Help database.

UNDERSTANDING LOTUS NOTES HELP

Help, like all information stored in Lotus Notes, is a database. That fact might not be obvious to you because you can access Help in so many ways. In other Lotus Notes databases, the only way to access the information contained in the database is to open the database. With Help, however, you don't have to double-click the database icon because you also can access it from the Help menu. Lotus Notes has two versions of Help: Notes Help and Notes Help Lite.

Notes Help is a larger database complete with navigators and is usually stored on the Domino server. Help is accessible to users who are constantly connected to the server.

Notes Help Lite is the database used for desktops or laptops that have minimal disk space available and whose operator might need to access Help when not connected to the Domino server. In Help Lite, you find the most frequently used Help topics. If you're using the Help Lite database, less information and fewer views are available. For instance, you won't have the option for the "Visual Index" view, discussed later in this lesson.

If you aren't sure which version you have, Help or Help Lite, look for the Help database icon on your workspace (see Figure 5.1). If the database icon says Help, you have the larger Help database. If the database icon says Help Lite, you have the smaller of the Help databases installed.

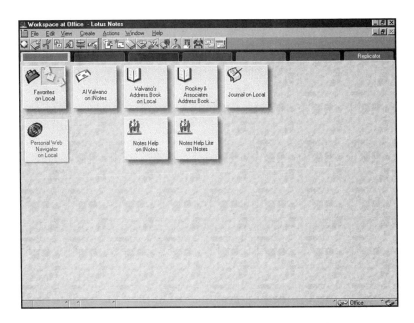

FIGURE 5.1   The Notes Help and Help Lite database icons.

If you don't see a Help database icon on your workspace, Notes adds a database icon the first time you choose Help from the menu. You also can add it yourself by opening the **File** menu and selecting **Database, Open**. Select **Notes Help** or **Notes Help Lite** from the database list on the server or locally if you are not connected to a server.

No Help Icon?   If you're connected to a Notes server, you don't really need the Help database icon. Help is still available to you through the Help menu.

After you add the database icon to your workspace, you can access the Help database by double-clicking its icon or by opening the Help menu, which is the method used for most Windows-based software.

TIP   **Quickly Accessing Help**   One of the fastest ways to access the Help database is to press the F1 key. This is a Windows standard shortcut key that also works in many other Windows software products. You can press F1 at any point, at any screen, in any database in Notes.

You move around and find information in the Help database the same way you move around and find information in other Lotus Notes databases—through views and searches. But as previously said, you can get to the information in the database in one of several ways:

- Use the menu **Help**, **Help Topics** to see the Help database table of contents.

- Press the **F1** key to see a list of hypertext options that help you answer the question "What do you want to do?"

- Use the **Guide Me** option for accessing context-sensitive Help.

- Double-click the Help database icon.

Figure 5.2 shows the Help database icon, as well as the Guide Me SmartIcon on the Notes workspace.

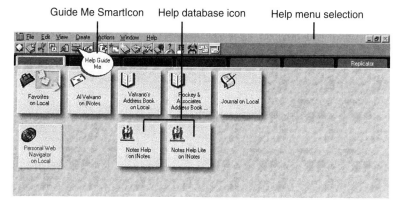

FIGURE 5.2   There are several ways to access Notes help.

USING THE HELP MENU

Take a look at how to use the menu to access Help. From your workspace, open the Help menu and select **Help Topics**. You'll see the main view of the Help database, called the Index view. The Index view is the default view, displaying the contents of the entire database (see Figure 5.3).

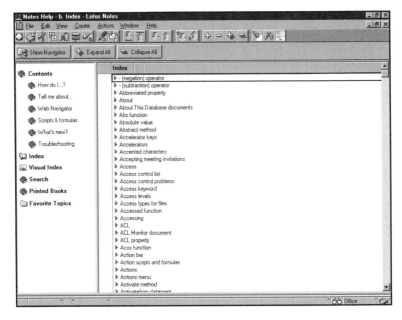

FIGURE 5.3   The Help database Index view.

This view takes advantage of collapsed and expanded views. Notice the little triangles that appear in front of some of the view topics? If the triangle is pointing to the right, the line of text you see is a category. A category is not an actual document; it is a categorization of the documents listed beneath it. To see the documents beneath a category, click the triangle. The triangle now points down, and the documents appear beneath the category.

To read a Help topic, simply double-click the document you want to read. Press **Esc** to return to the Index view.

When the triangle points down, this is an *expanded* view. One way of expanding and collapsing views is to click the triangle. If the category is collapsed, clicking expands it. If the category is expanded, clicking collapses it. You also can use the SmartIcons located on the toolbar to expand and collapse views. See the following minitable for descriptions of the icons.

Icon	Description
	Expands the category you currently have highlighted
	Collapses the category you currently have highlighted
	Expands all categories in the database
	Collapses all categories in the database

In the left panel of the Index view are navigators to other available views. Here's a quick summary of what these Help views provide:

- **How do I . . . ?**   Contains a list of task-oriented functions such as Ways to address mail.

- **Tell me about . . .**   Provides shortcuts, notes, database design, and management concepts.

- **Web Navigator**   Contains Help information on using the Web Navigator database to access the web.

- **Scripts and Formulas**   Contains information on LotusScript and the Notes formula language used in the development of databases.

- **What's new?**   Contains information about Lotus Notes Release 4.6 for users of previous versions.

- **Troubleshooting**   Lists and answers common questions, meanings of error messages, and available web sites for information about Notes.

- **Index**   Displays a list of categorized Help topics. This is the default view for the database.

- **Visual Index**   Graphically displays Help topics. This feature is available only in the Help version of Notes Help, not in the Help Lite version.

- **Search**   Lists topics alphabetically, without categories.

- **Printed Books**   Contains Notes documentation in book form, such as the Programmers Guide and User Guide.

- **Favorite Topics**   Populate this folder with help pages you frequently access.

As you select a view navigator on the *left* of your screen, the contents change on the *right* of your screen. Each time you change views, you can navigate to another view or press the **Esc** key to return to your workspace. Take a minute and try some of the navigators.

You can disable the navigator by clicking the **Navigator** button on the Action bar. This takes you to the Folders view. Clicking the Navigator button a second time takes you back to the navigator.

USING THE VISUAL INDEX

The Visual Index view displays the contents of the database with navigators, as shown in Figure 5.4. This view is available only if you are using the Help version available on the Notes server. To see the Visual Index view:

1. Click the **Visual Index** navigator. The Visual Index view displays navigators on the left pane of your screen, representing topics (see Figure 5.4). Investigate the Workspace Management navigator.

2. Click the **Workspace Management** navigator.

3. A picture of the workspace appears. Tiny yellow bubbles act as *hotspots* to lead you to help on a given topic.

4. Click the tiny yellow bubble that points to the My Work tab in the picture of the workspace. The Entering a name on a Workspace tab Help topic appears.

5. Click the **Go Back** button in the Action bar to return to the Workspace navigator. Click again to return to the Visual Index view and once again to return to the Index view.

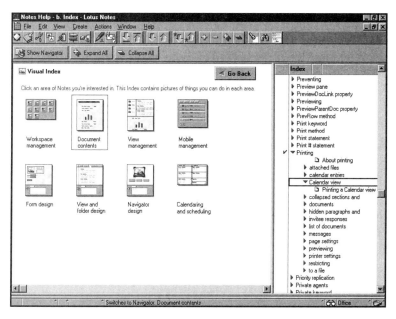

FIGURE 5.4 The Help database Visual Index view.

PERFORMING SEARCHES

There are two ways to search for information in the Help database—Quick Search and Guide Me. Quick Search searches through the titles of the Lotus Notes Help documents but not through the contents of the documents. Quick Search works only if your view is expanded. Instead of scrolling or using the Page Down key, you can use Quick Search to move quickly through the database screens.

For example, if you want to find information on printing from the
Index view, you need only press the letter **P** on your keyboard. The
Quick Search dialog box appears, as shown in Figure 5.5.

Figure 5.5   Quick search dialog box.

After the dialog box appears, you can type the first letter of a
word, the first part of a word, or the entire word for which you
want to search. If you type only the letter **P** and click **OK**, the
first document title that starts with the letter P displays highlighted. If you type the entire word **Print**, the search finds the
first document title that starts with the word Print.

Another way to search a database is to search the database document contents for words not included in the title of the document. The Help database has a Search view for that purpose. You
can use this view to search for a specific word or phrase. You can
access the Search view by clicking the **Search** navigator located
in the Main, or Index view. To use the Search view and search for
a word or phrase in the Help database:

1. Click the **Search** navigator.

2. Click the **Show Search Bar** button on the Action bar.
   The Search bar is under the toolbar.

Search Bar   A set of tools that help you find information
in Lotus Notes databases. You can use the Search bar in
most of your databases in Lotus Notes. You should expand your views to search all documents in the database.

3. Click the text box of the Search bar.

4. Type the word or phrase you want to search for: Type
   mail.

5. Click the **Search** button.

6. The search results appear in the right pane of the Help window. To access any of the search results documents, simply double-click the document in the right pane of your screen. Notice that the number of documents found that meet your search criteria is indicated on the status bar.

7. To return to the Index view of Help, click the **Index** navigator.

8. To refresh your screen, click the **Reset** button located on the Action bar. The word **mail** remains in your Search bar text box. You can replace this the next time you do a search for another topic or phrase.

9. To exit the Help database, press the **Esc** key.

WORKING WITH GUIDE ME

Another way to access Help is to use the context-sensitive Guide Me feature of Lotus Notes. To activate Guide Me, press the **F1** key. When you use this key, instead of showing you the views just discussed, Lotus Notes displays a list of topics asking you **What do you want to do?** followed by topics that you can double-click to search how to perform tasks. You can use this at any time from any place while working in Lotus Notes:

1. Click the **Inbox** navigator of your Lotus Notes Mail database.

2. Press the key for help.

3. A screen appears, asking **What do you want to do?** Double-click **Print**. A list of print topics appears.

4. Double-click **Print one document?**.

5. Now you can read the instructions for printing a document. To exit this screen and the Mail database, press the **Esc** key until you return to your workspace.

Getting Additional Help for Mobile Users

If you're a mobile user or responsible for helping mobile users, you might want to access the Notes Mobile Survival Kit. This database contains troubleshooting tips and general information on modems, remote Notes, and wireless issues. The Notes Mobile Survival Kit has the latest modem command files, pager files, and script files. It also contains pre-support call questions that you should check before you call for technical support.

The Notes Mobile Survival Kit (Mod_Surv.Nsf) may be stored on your Lotus Notes server. Check with your Notes administrator to get help accessing or replicating this database. You also can access the Notes survival database through a web browser at **http://www.notes.net/mod_surv**.

In this lesson, you learned how to access and use Lotus Notes Help and how to search for information in the Help database. In the next lesson, you'll learn how to create mail messages.

CREATING MAIL

In this lesson, you learn about email, how to create and address a mail message, and about email etiquette.

HOW LOTUS NOTES MAIL WORKS

Email is short for electronic mail. Simply put, it's mail that you create on your computer and send to someone over a network or the Internet. With Lotus Notes, you create email in a form called the mail memo form. When you click the **Send** button, the mail travels to the server and into the mailbox of the addressee(s). When they open their mail, they see the mail you sent. With Lotus Notes, the Domino server stores all the mailboxes of the users on that server.

If your Domino server has access to the Internet, you can send mail to people on the Internet. Mail that you send to the Internet first travels to your Domino server and then to the Internet. This might happen immediately or it might be on a scheduled basis, depending on how your administrator has configured your Domino server. If your server doesn't have access to the Internet, it's possible for you to set up Notes to send Internet mail directly from your computer.

USING EMAIL ETIQUETTE

Because so many people use email, it's necessary to follow certain "rules" concerning what is proper or acceptable—*email etiquette.*

Check out these points of etiquette so you can responsibly and effectively use Lotus Notes Mail:

- *Always include information in the subject line*   Don't send email without including a clear and concise description of your message in the Subject line. It lets your recipients know what the message is about before they open it.

- *Beware of the written word*   Although email is fairly secure, it's not entirely secure. Someone might forward your message to others. Also, sarcasm doesn't translate well from the spoken word to the written word. You might be taken seriously or offend someone when you were only joking.

- *Send meaningful email*   Some companies do not allow any personal use of email. Even if they do, you should still be thoughtful about the number of messages you send people and the importance of those messages. People might not appreciate unsolicited jokes, thoughts for the day, gossip, and cartoons.

- *Give thought to sending attachments*   You can attach files from other programs within your Lotus Notes Mail. However, it takes time for the recipient to open and read an attachment. Send an attachment only if the recipient needs to make changes to or have a copy of that file for his records or the file is too large to cut, copy, and paste into your mail memo. Also, include information in your memo so the receiver knows what the file contains before he opens it.

- *Don't send email to the world*   Don't create large distribution lists. If you need to distribute information to a large group of people, ask your Notes administrator for possible alternatives. A discussion database application or a repository application might be better for sharing information.

- *DON'T USE ALL CAPS*   Typing in all uppercase letters implies that you're shouting.

- *Use Reply to All*   When you answer an email message that includes several names in the To or cc fields, use the Reply to All feature if your answer would be of use to all those people. Otherwise, some people will be dropped from the conversation and you (or the person to whom you're replying) will have to resend the reply to them. Conversely, don't use Reply to All if you only need to respond to the sender.

- *Keep your messages short*   The shorter the better. Some people often skip over email when the message contains more than a screen full of information.

- *Remember that you are using company property*   Unlike mail that's sent through the post office, your email is company property. Unless your company policy allows it, email topics that are personal, not work related, or highly confidential should not be exchanged over the company's email system.

- *Don't print out your Inbox*   This is more a common sense than an etiquette issue. If you print your email for reading purposes, aren't you defeating the purpose?

Don't Risk Your Job!   Remember that many large corporations have company policies regarding email; ask your company for a copy of these policies so you don't violate any rules that might cause problems for you at work.

CREATING A MAIL MESSAGE

You can start a mail message from several places in Lotus Notes.

- If you are on the workspace, choose **Create**, **Mail**, **Memo** or click the **Create Mail Memo** SmartIcon.

- If you are on the workspace and you have selected your mail database icon, choose **Create**, **Memo**.

- If you have opened your mail database and can see the Action bar, click the **New Memo** button.

- Click the **Mail** icon on the status bar and choose **Create Memo**.

A new mail memo appears, ready for you to enter the name(s) of the recipient(s), a subject, and the message.

USING THE ADDRESS OPTIONS

When the New Memo window opens, you see several *fields* that you must complete (see Figure 6.1). A field holds a piece of information stored in the database. Square brackets mark the fields where you enter text.

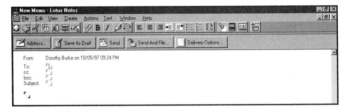

FIGURE 6.1   A new mail memo.

Entering text in Lotus Notes fields is like typing in a word processor. You can use the Backspace and Delete keys to remove unwanted text. You can move the insertion point (cursor) by using the arrow keys or by clicking with the mouse. You can insert text wherever you place the cursor.

When you need to move your insertion point to the next field, press the **Tab** key or click the field.

The first field to complete on your memo is the To field. This is where you put the name of the person or the names of people who will receive your message. You can enter this information by using the *Quick address* option or by looking up names in the address books.

In the cc (carbon copy) field, enter the names of people you want to receive a copy of the message you send to the recipient. The names in the cc field appear on the recipient's message, and all these people also see the cc names.

Use the bcc (blind carbon copy) field to send hidden copy. The name of the bcc recipient does not appear on any other messages; only you and the person you bcc know he received a copy. If you put two names in the bcc field, those two people don't know that the other received the message.

USING THE QUICK ADDRESS OPTION

The Quick Address option saves you work. When you type the first letter of a name in the To field, Quick Address finds and enters the full name of the first person in your address book that starts with that letter. For example, when you type **P**, Notes fills in the name Paul Abbott. Then, as you enter the second letter, **e**, Notes finds and enters Peter Anderson, and so on.

Quick Address also accepts last names. When you enter the beginning letter(s) of the last name and press **Tab** to go to the next field, Notes finds the name and reverses the order when it fills in the field. So, when you type **A**, Notes might find Ann Rutherford, but when you type **b** and press **Tab**, Notes should locate the last name Abbott and insert Paul Abbott in the address field.

Quick Address only works if the name of the recipient is in an address book. Otherwise, you must type the full name and address of the person.

Address Book   A database that contains the names and electronic mail addresses of all the users with whom you communicate through email. Lotus Notes Mail has two address books: Personal and Public. The Personal Address Book is stored on your local drive and usually has your last name as the title (such as "Burke's Address Book"), whereas the Public Address Book is on the server and usually has the name of your company (such as "MCP Corporation's Address Book"). Lesson 9 covers address books in detail.

If you want to address the memo to more than one person, separate the names with commas. Quick Address works for each name.

ADDRESSING FROM THE ADDRESS BOOK

If you aren't sure of a person's last name or the spelling of his
name, you can look him up in the address book. You can choose
to insert the person's name into the To, cc, or bcc fields. To use an
address book, follow these steps:

1. Click the **Address** button on the Action toolbar.

   When the Mail Address dialog box appears, you'll see a
   list of names from your Personal Address Book (see Figure
   6.2). At this point, your Personal Address Book is probably
   empty. To access the Public Address Book, click the drop-
   down menu and select the name of your Public Address
   Book. Remember, you must be able to connect to the
   server to access the Public Address Book.

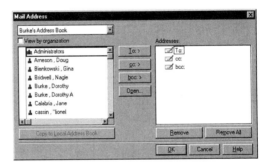

FIGURE 6.2   The Mail Address dialog box.

2. Select the name of the person that you need from the
   available list of names (to select more than one name,
   click the margin in front of each name to place a check
   mark there). You can use the scrollbar to move up or
   down the list.

3. Click the **To**, **cc**, or **bcc** button, depending on which address field you want to fill.

4. Repeat the last two steps for each name you want to enter.

5. Click **OK**.

FILLING IN THE MAIL MESSAGE DOCUMENT

Complete the Subject field by entering a short description of your memo in this field, similar to a headline for a newspaper article. Every time someone replies to your message, the reply memo shows the same subject, which appears on all replies and replies to replies.

After completing the Subject field, type your mail message in the Body field. When you finish typing your message, you should spell check before you mail it. If you feel you don't need to spell check the message, click the **Send** button on the Action bar to send your mail (see Figure 6.3).

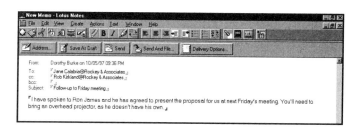

FIGURE 6.3   A completed mail message, ready to send.

USING SPELL CHECK

Spell Check compares your text against a stored spelling dictionary of tens of thousands of words. If any of your words aren't in the spelling dictionary, Spell Check alerts you that the word is possibly misspelled. In addition to your misspellings and typos, Spell Check also alerts you to proper names and unusual words that might be spelled correctly but are not in the spelling dictionary.

Lotus Notes looks in two dictionaries for correctly spelled words. The main dictionary is extensive, covering most of the common words in American English. Proper names, acronyms, and business jargon not included in the main dictionary are then looked for in your user dictionary. The user dictionary is one to which you can add.

Spell Check also reports duplicate words, such as "the the," but it won't look at single-character words such as "a" and "I" or words that are longer than 64 letters. It also ignores text that doesn't have any letters, such as the number 1,200,543.

When you want to check the spelling in your message, you must be in edit mode. Edit mode enables you to change the text in the document in which you are currently working. When you're *creating* a new mail message, you're automatically in edit mode.

To run Spell Check, follow these steps:

1. Choose **Edit, Check Spelling** or click the **Check Spelling** SmartIcon. The Spell Check dialog box appears, as shown in Figure 6.4.

FIGURE 6.4 The Spell Check dialog box.

2. When Spell Check finds a word it doesn't recognize, choose one of the following options:

    Skip Ignores the misspelling and goes on to the next word. Use this option when the word is spelled correctly.

Skip All   Tells Notes to ignore all the instances of this word in the message. This is useful when a correctly spelled proper name crops up several times in a memo.

Define   Enables you to add the word to your user dictionary. Once added, Spell Check recognizes this word as correctly spelled.

Replace   Enables you to change an incorrect spelling to a correct one. If the correct spelling of the word shows up in the Guess box, click the correct guess and then the **Replace** button. If Spell Check provides no suggestions and you know the correct spelling, click the **Replace** box and make the correction by deleting or adding characters. Then, click **Replace** to make the change in your message.

3. Once the Spell Check ends, click **Done**.

By default, Spell Check checks your entire mail message. If you want to Spell Check one word or a paragraph, select the word or text with your mouse; then start the Spell Check, as previously mentioned.

TIP   **Selecting Text**   Place your mouse pointer to the left of the word(s) you want to select, hold down the left mouse button, and drag the mouse across the word(s). Release the mouse when the word(s) you want selected appears highlighted. To deselect the text, click anywhere in the window.

Running Spell Check doesn't guarantee a perfect mail message. If you accidentally type the word "form" when you wanted to type "from," Spell Check won't catch it because "form" is a word in the dictionary. Also, Spell Check doesn't catch incorrect punctuation or missing words. There is also a possibility that a word was not added correctly to the user dictionary. To change words that you added to your user dictionary, follow these steps:

1. Choose **File**, **Tools**, **User Preferences**. In the User Preferences dialog box (see Figure 6.5), click the **User Dictionary** button.

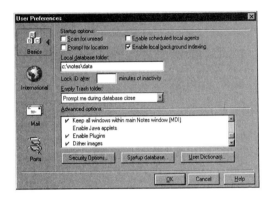

FIGURE 6.5   The User Preferences dialog box.

2. You can then make any of the following changes:

   • To delete the incorrectly spelled word, select it and click **Delete**.

   • To change a misspelled word, select it from the list, enter the correct spelling in the small text box at the bottom of the dialog box, and then click **Update**.

   • To add a word, enter it in the small text box and click **Add**.

3. When you finish, click **OK**. Then, click **OK** to close the User Preferences dialog box.

CREATING MEMOS FROM CALENDAR ENTRIES AND TASKS

You don't have to be in the Inbox view to send a mail message. You might be looking at a Calendar entry or a Task and decide to send a mail message relating to that document. Do the following to create a mail memo from a Calendar entry or Task:

1. Select or open the calendar entry or task you want to use.

2. Choose **Actions, Copy Into, New Memo** from the menu.

3. The memo appears with the Subject field, repeating the name of the calendar entry or task and some brief information in the body field. Make any necessary modifications to the memo.

4. Send the message.

You'll learn more about working with the Calendar in Lessons 18 and 19 and about creating Tasks in Lesson 17.

In this lesson, you learned some pointers for proper use of email and how to fill out a mail message, how to use your word processor to create mail messages, and how to create mail messages from Calendar entries and tasks. In the next lesson, you will learn how to format text.

FORMATTING TEXT

In this lesson, you learn about rich text fields, formatting text and setting paragraph attributes, and adding special characters to your mail messages.

UNDERSTANDING RICH TEXT FIELDS

Until now, most of the fields you've been working with have been *text* fields. In a text field, you can enter text or numbers, but you can't format the text. To format text is to make your text bold, italic, underlined, larger or smaller, or a different typeface.

The body field of the mail memo is a different kind of text field—a *rich text field*. In that field, you can format text. You also can add graphics, attachments, objects, hotspots, pop-ups, special characters, and tables to this field.

 TIP **No Size Limit** A rich text field has virtually no size limit. If your message is longer than one screen, however, consider typing your message in a word processing program. You can then attach this file to your mail message.

You can identify a rich text field by looking at the Lotus Notes status bar. When your insertion point (cursor) is in a rich text field, the font name, font size, and named style assigned to that field appear on the status bar. Additionally, red square brackets surround the field. Figure 7.1 shows the mail memo form with the cursor in the body field.

Text Bold   Text Italic   Text Permanent Pen   A rich text field

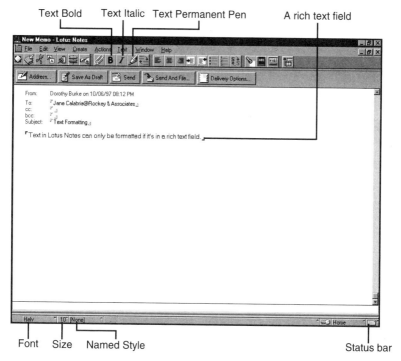

Font   Size   Named Style   Status bar

FIGURE 7.1   The status bar indicates a rich text field.

METHODS OF FORMATTING TEXT

To change your text's appearance, you can add headings, sub-headings, bullets, numbers, bold, and italics. You also can under-line your text, change the fonts and colors, and use strikethrough, superscript, and subscript. You can combine these formatting options, such as ***bold and italic***, or **bold and underlined**, or *italic and underlined*.

You format text by using one of two methods:

- Type all your text. Then, select the text you want to for-mat and apply your formatting options to the selected text.

- Choose the formatting options first and then type the text. The text you type is formatted, as specified. To resume the previous formatting or turn off the formatting option, you must set the formatting options again. The new options apply to any text you type thereafter.

CHANGING TEXT FORMATS

As with most word processing programs, you can set text formatting options by using the toolbar, the menu bar, or keystrokes.

My Formatting Is Lost!   If you send mail to the Internet, many of the Notes formatting options do not translate. To ensure that your Internet recipient can read your Notes mail, stick with the Notes default font and create a "plain text" message. If you send mail to a Notes Mail user through the Internet, you can preserve your Notes formatting by selecting **Actions, Special Options** and placing a check mark in the box labeled **I am sending this Notes document to other mail user(s) through the Internet**. Use this option only when you are sending to another Notes user.

On the toolbar, there are two SmartIcons for formatting text— Text Bold and Text Italic (refer to Figure 7.1). Click either one or both to apply bold and italic attributes to selected text or the text you are about to type. Click the same buttons again to turn off these attributes.

The Text menu offers choices of Normal Text, Italic, Bold, Underline, and Strikethrough. Select **Enlarge Size** to make the text larger or **Reduce Size** to make it smaller. Select the text to which you want to apply the attribute(s), or position your insertion point where you want the attribute to start, and then choose **Text** from the menu and the attribute you want to apply.

Strikethrough Use this attribute to show text that has been struck from a document, ~~such as this~~. Use **Superscript** to place text above the line, such as a trademark™ notation, and **Subscript** to place text below the line, such as in the H_2O chemical symbol.

To use keystrokes to apply formatting attributes to selected text or text you are about to type, press **Ctrl+T** for normal text, **Ctrl+I** for italic, **Ctrl+B** for bold, **Ctrl+U** for underline, **F2** to enlarge the size, and **Shift+F2** to reduce the size.

The formatting choices on the status bar enable you to quickly select a font, size, or style. Helvetica is the default font Lotus Notes uses, so the font button usually says **Helv** on it. That changes, however, when you select a new font. The Size and Named Style buttons also change to reflect the formatting applied to the currently selected text or the text where your insertion point is. To use the status bar buttons, select the text to be formatted or place your insertion point where you want to type text with the new format and then click one of the buttons on the Status bar. Make your choice from the pop-up menu that appears (see Figure 7.2).

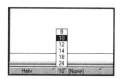

FIGURE 7.2 The Font Size pop-up menu on the status bar.

Lotus Notes also offers text formatting options through the Text Properties box. To open the Text Properties box, click the **Properties** SmartIcon on the toolbar or choose **Text**, **Text Properties** from the menu or right-click the text and choose **Text Properties** from the shortcut menu. The Text Properties box appears, as shown in Figure 7.3.

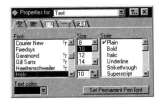

FIGURE 7.3   The Text Properties box with the Font tab selected.

Select the typeface you want to use from the Font list, the point size from the Size list (or enter a size in the text box below the Size list), and the font style—such as bold, italic, and underline—from the Style list. To apply a text color, select one from the Text Color drop-down list. As you make your selections, Notes immediately applies them to selected text. You don't have to close the Properties box as you do a dialog box (refer to Lesson 3 to learn more about using the Properties box); you can leave it open as you apply attributes to different parts of your message text.

TIP   **Be Conservative**   Lotus Notes displays your entire list of fonts, but don't use them all in the same mail message. Many available computer fonts are decorative and fine to use for a couple of words but difficult to read in large blocks of text. Additionally, not everyone shares the fonts you have on your computer, and they might not be able to see or read the text when they receive your memo.

COLOR

One of the best ways to add emphasis and emotion to your text is with color. To add color to text, choose **Text**, **Color** from the menu bar, and then select a color name from the list. To see more color choices, click the **Other** button. The Properties box opens; you can choose a color from the Text color drop-down list by clicking the color swatch you want to apply to the text or by opening the Properties box and then selecting the color from the Text Color drop-down list.

THE PERMANENT PEN

The permanent pen enables you to add text in another color or font. This is especially useful for making comments that contrast with the regular text. Why would you use this instead of changing the text attributes the normal way? With the permanent pen, you don't have to change the text formatting every time you move the cursor.

To turn on the permanent pen, choose **Text**, **Permanent Pen** or click the **Permanent Pen** SmartIcon. Then, type the text you want to appear in the permanent pen style. To stop the permanent pen style, click the **Permanent Pen** SmartIcon again.

To set the look of the permanent pen, open the Text Properties box (refer to Figure 7.3). Select the first tab (labeled **AZ**). Make all of your formatting selections for the permanent pen (make sure you don't have any text selected before you do this). Click **Set Permanent Pen Font**.

FORMATTING PARAGRAPHS

Lotus Notes provides many tools for paragraph formatting. A paragraph, as defined in word processing, is any text that ends with a hard return (Enter). When you want to set the paragraph formatting (indent, alignment, bullets, or numbers), select the paragraphs you want to affect or place your insertion point where you want to enter text using the new format.

PARAGRAPH ALIGNMENT

You can change the horizontal *alignment* of a paragraph, as described in Table 7.1.

TABLE 7.1 PARAGRAPH ALIGNMENT

ALIGNMENT	DESCRIPTION
Flush left	Aligns text to left margin; text is ragged on right margin.

ALIGNMENT	DESCRIPTION
Flush right	Aligns text on right margin; text is ragged on left margin.
Center	Centers text between left and right margins.
Justified	Aligns text on both right and left margins.
No wrap	Turns off word wrapping and displays text on one line.

To choose alignment, click the appropriate SmartIcon (see Figure 7.4), choose **Text**, **Align Paragragh** from the menu, or select one of the alignment options on the Paragraph tab of the Text Properties box (see Figure 7.5).

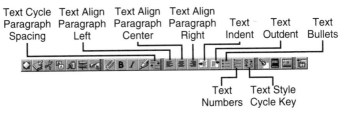

FIGURE 7.4 SmartIcons for selecting paragraph formatting.

FIGURE 7.5 The Text Properties box with the Alignment tab selected.

PARAGRAPH INDENTATION

Lotus Notes gives you a number of ways to *indent* paragraphs. Indenting moves the beginning of the first line of the paragraph to the right by a specified amount. Outdenting moves the beginning of the first line of the paragraph to the left by a specified amount (also referred to as a hanging paragraph). To indent or outdent a paragraph, use the **Text Indent** or **Text Outdent** SmartIcons (refer to Figure 7.4), choose **Text, Indent** or **Text, Outdent** from the menu, press **F8** to indent or **Shift+F8** to outdent, or select the appropriate **First Line** option on the Alignment tab of the Text Properties box (refer to Figure 7.5).

You also can use the ruler above the open message to set indents by doing the following:

1. Select the paragraph or paragraphs to indent.

2. Choose **View**, **Ruler**. The ruler appears above the open message (see Figure 7.6).

3. Drag the upper pentagon pointer to where you want the first line of the paragraph(s) to start, drag the lower pentagon pointer to where you want the remaining lines of the selected paragraph(s) to start or drag the rectangle that sits beneath the pentagons to adjust all lines at once. If you drag the top or the bottom pentagon and meant to take both, simply double-click the one you moved. This forces the pentagons together again.

First line indent pentagon

Remaining text indent pentagon

FIGURE 7.6   Ruler with indent pentagons.

PARAGRAPH SPACING

You can set the *spacing* between lines in a paragraph, as well as the amount of space before and after paragraphs. Every time you click the **Text Cycle Paragraph Spacing** SmartIcon, the spacing below each paragraph cycles between Single, 1¹/₂, and Double. Choosing **Text**, **Spacing** also changes the spacing below the paragraph. To make more specific selections, open the Text Properties box and select the **Alignment** tab. The Spacing options include Interline (the spacing between lines of text within the paragraph), Above (the space above the paragraph), and Below (the space after the paragraph).

BULLETS AND NUMBERS

You can convert text in existing paragraphs to a bulleted or numbered list simply by selecting the paragraphs and then clicking the **Text Bullets** or **Text Numbers** SmartIcon on the toolbar. Each paragraph becomes a separate bullet or number in the listing. Or you can click the SmartIcon and begin typing the text. Each time you press **Enter**, a new bullet or the next number in sequence appears.

If the Text Properties box is open, select the **Alignment** tab and click the List option you want to apply—bullets or numbering. You also can set bullets or numbering by choosing **Text**, **Bullets** or **Text**, **Numbers** from the menu.

 TIP   **Automatic Renumbering**   If you decide you don't need one of the items in your numbered list, simply delete it, and Notes automatically renumbers the list, if necessary.

SETTING TABS

Tabs are set every 1/2 inch in Lotus Notes, but sometimes you need to set your own tabs. You can set tabs from the Text Properties box or from the ruler.

From the Text Properties box, do the following:

1. Select the paragraph(s) for which you want to set tabs.

2. Choose **Text**, **Text Properties**, and then click the **Page** tab (see Figure 7.7).

FIGURE 7.7   The Text Properties box with the Page tab selected.

3. In the Tabs drop-down list box, choose one of the following:

   • *Individually Set*   Enter the tab stops you want (if you enter more than one, separate them with semicolons).

   • *Evenly Spaced*   Enter the interval between tab stops. Always enter the numbers followed by the inch mark (").

4. (**Optional**) If you want to enter left, right, center, or decimal tabs, type an L, R, C, or D before the number (such as L1").

To set tabs by using the ruler, follow these steps:

1. Select the paragraph(s) to which you want to add tabs.

2. If you don't see the ruler, choose **View**, **Ruler**.

3. On the ruler (see Figure 7.8), click where you want a left tab, right-click where you want a right tab, press **Shift** and click where you want a decimal tab, and press **Shift** and right-click where you want a centered tab.

To remove a tab from the ruler, click it. To change the type of the tab, right-click the tab and select a tab type.

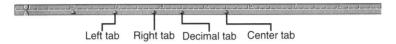

Left tab   Right tab   Decimal tab   Center tab

Figure 7.8   The ruler, showing tab stops.

In this lesson, you learned about rich text fields and how to format text and paragraphs. You also learned how to apply the permanent pen. In the next lesson, you will learn to add sections and tables to your memos.

ADVANCED FORMATTING

In this lesson, you learn how to improve the appearance and readability of your mail memos by adding sections, tables, horizontal lines, and pictures.

CREATING SECTIONS

Sections are helpful in making large documents more manageable. You can gather all the information on one topic into a section. Sections collapse into one-line paragraphs or expand to display all the text in the section, so a reader doesn't have to read sections that aren't of any interest to them.

A section is identified by a small triangle that appears to the left of the section head. To read a section, you must first expand it. Do this by clicking the triangle (called a *twistee*). Clicking the twistee again collapses the section. To expand all the sections in a document, choose **View**, **Expand All Sections** from the menu. To collapse all sections, choose **View**, **Collapse All Sections** from the menu. Figure 8.1 shows a document with an expanded section.

To create a section in your message:

1. Create a new mail message. Type several paragraphs in the body field.

2. Select the paragraph or paragraphs you want to make into a section.

3. Choose **Create**, **Section** from the menu.

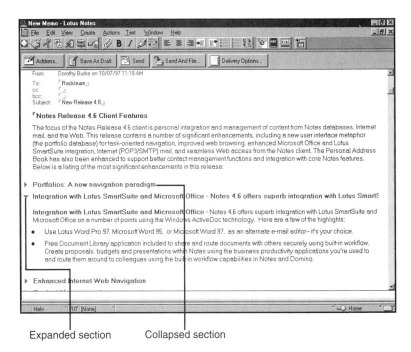

Expanded section   Collapsed section

FIGURE 8.1   A mail memo with collapsed and expanded sections.

The first paragraph of the section becomes the section title. If you want to change it, follow these steps:

1. Click the section title.

2. Choose **Section Properties** from the menu (see Figure 8.2).

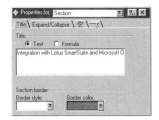

FIGURE 8.2   The Section Properties box with the Title tab selected.

3. Click the **Title** tab.

4. Select **Text**, and then replace the text in the Title box with the section title you want.

5. Under Section Border, choose a Border Style from the list box and a Border Color from the list box.

6. If you want to hide the title of the section when it expands, click the **Expand/Collapse** tab, and check **Hide Title When Expanded** (see Figure 8.3).

FIGURE 8.3   The Section Properties box with the Expand/Collapse tab selected.

If you want to format the section title, select it and choose **Section**, **Section Properties**. Click the **Font** tab (AZ); then select the font, size, style, and color you want for the section title.

To move a section from one part of a document to another, select the section and choose **Edit**, **Cut** (or click the **Edit Cut** SmartIcon or press **Ctrl+X**). Position your cursor where you want the section to appear. Choose **Edit**, **Paste** (or click the **Edit Paste** SmartIcon or press **Ctrl+V**).

When you want to remove a section but still want to keep all the text in the section, select the section and choose **Section**, **Remove Section** from the menu. If you want to remove the section and all its text, however, choose **Edit**, **Clear** or press the **Delete** key.

INSERTING TABLES

Tables offer an excellent way to organize data, and you can easily add tables to your mail messages. Figure 8.4 shows a mail message with a table inserted.

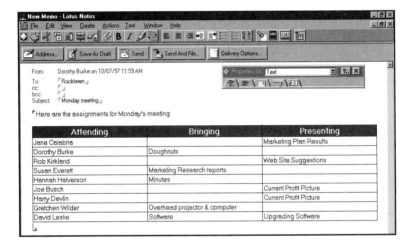

FIGURE 8.4   A mail message with a table inserted.

To insert a table in your mail message:

1. Create a new memo.

2. Position your cursor in the body field where you want the table to appear.

3. Choose **Create**, **Table** or click the **Create Table** SmartIcon. The Create Table dialog box appears (see Figure 8.5).

4. Enter the number of Rows and Columns you want in your table.

5. Click **OK**.

FIGURE 8.5   The Create Table dialog box.

INSERTING, DELETING, COPYING, AND MOVING COLUMNS AND ROWS

If you didn't specify the correct number of columns or rows when you created the table, you can insert or delete columns or rows.

To insert one column or row:

1. Click the column or row where you want to insert a new one. New columns appear to the left of the column your cursor is in; new rows appear above the row your cursor is in.

2. Choose **Table**, **Insert Column** or **Table**, **Insert Row** from the menu (or click the **Table Insert Row** SmartIcon to add a row).

To add a row at the bottom of the table or a column at the right of the table, choose **Table**, **Append Row** or **Table**, **Append Column** from the menu.

To add more than one column or row, position your cursor and choose **Table**, **Insert Special**. Specify the number of columns or rows you want to add and choose **Column(s)** or **Row(s)**. Click **Insert** (see Figure 8.6).

FIGURE 8.6   The Insert Row/Column dialog box.

To delete a column or row, click the row or column you want to remove. **Choose Table, Delete Selected Column(s)** or **Table, Delete Selected Row(s)** (or click the **Table Delete Selected Row(s)** SmartIcon). Click **Yes** to confirm the deletion. Remember—deleting a column or row also deletes all the text in that column or row.

To delete several columns or rows, place your cursor in the first column or row of the ones you want to delete. Choose **Table, Delete Special**. Specify the number of columns or rows you want to delete, select **Columns(s)** or **Row(s)**, and click **Delete**. Choose **Yes** to confirm the deletion.

Delete the Text, Not the Table! You don't have to delete columns or rows to delete the text. If you want to leave your columns and rows intact, select the text and choose **Edit, Clear**, or press **Delete**.

You can use **Edit, Copy** (or click the **Edit Copy** SmartIcon or press **Ctrl+C**) to copy rows or columns of data in a table. **Edit, Cut** (or click the **Edit Cut** SmartIcon or press **Ctrl+X**) removes selected columns or rows and stores them in the Clipboard. You can then use **Edit, Paste** (or click the **Edit Paste** SmartIcon or press **Ctrl+V**) to place the columns in a new position (where you have your cursor).

FORMATTING TABLES

You also can control how your table looks. You can put borders around the outside of the table or around each cell. You can set the width of the columns and the space between columns and rows, and you can determine the overall width of the table.

To set borders on the table:

1. Select the cells of the table to which you want to add borders.

2. Choose **Table**, **Table Properties** from the menu or click the **Table Properties** SmartIcon. Figure 8.7 shows the Table Properties box.

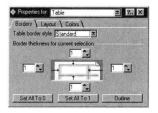

FIGURE 8.7   The Table Properties box with the Borders tab selected.

3. Click the **Borders** tab. You can choose how you want your borders to look:

   • To set the type of lines you want to use as borders for your cells, choose **Standard**, **Extruded**, or **Embossed** from the Table Border Style list box.

   • Click **Outline** to set the borders for only the outside lines of the current selection.

   • To set the borders on all sides to single, click the **Set All to 1** button.

   • To not have any borders, click the **Set All to 0** button.

   • To set the sides individually, specify the number of lines for each side (0 equals none, 1 equals single, 2 equals double, and so on).

To set the overall width of the table so the column widths adjust to fit the table in the window, do the following:

1. Click anywhere in the table.

2. Choose **Table**, **Table Properties** from the menu or click the **Table Properties** SmartIcon. The Table Properties box appears.

3. Click the **Layout** tab.

4. Select **Fit Table Width to Window** to automatically size the table to fit the window.

To change the margins and spacing between columns or rows or to make the table fit to a window:

1. Click anywhere in the table.

2. Choose **Table**, **Table Properties** from the menu or click the **Table Properties** SmartIcon.

3. Click the **Layout** tab (see Figure 8.8).

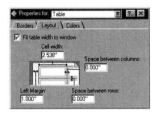

FIGURE 8.8   The Table Properties box with the Layout tab selected.

4. Set any of the following layout features:

- To set the left margin of the table, enter a new value in the Left Margin box.

- To set the spacing between the columns and rows, enter a new value in Space Between Columns and/or Space Between Rows.

- To change the column width, remove the check mark from Fit Table Width to Window and enter the new width in the Cell Width box.

You also can set the column width by using the ruler:

1. Click the column you want to modify.

2. If you don't see the ruler, choose **View**, **Ruler** from the menu.

3. The column has two thin bar pointers on the ruler. Drag the first one to show where the column starts; drag the second one to where the column ends.

You add color to the cells in your table or to the entire table by doing the following:

1. Select the cell or cells you want to color.

2. Choose **Table**, **Table Properties** from the menu or click the **Table Properties** SmartIcon.

3. Click the **Colors** tab.

4. Select the color you want to use from the Backgound Color drop-down list.

5. If you want the same background for all the cells in the table, click **Apply to Entire Table**.

6. If you want the cell background to be transparent, click **Make Transparent**.

In this lesson, you learned how to create sections in your mail messages. You also learned how to add and format tables. In the next lesson, you will learn about address books.

USING THE ADDRESS BOOKS

In this lesson, you learn about the two address books found in Lotus Notes—the Public Address Book and the Personal Address Book.

WHAT IS THE ADDRESS BOOK?

Like mail, address books are databases. You store your email addresses in Lotus Notes address books. In Lesson 6, you used the Public Address Book to add names to a mail memo. Lotus Notes has at least two address books available for your use—the Personal Address Book and the company or Public Address Book (see Figure 9.1).

Public Address Book   Personal Address Book

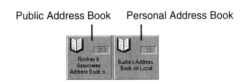

FIGURE 9.1 The address book icons.

Your *Personal Address Book* has your name on it and is empty until you add people to it. In contrast, the *Public Address Book* contains the addresses of employees in your company who use Lotus Notes Mail, and it has your company's name on it. Your Lotus Notes administrator maintains this address book.

USING THE PUBLIC ADDRESS BOOK

When your company or organization first sets up Lotus Notes, they establish a Public Address Book, which includes the address of everyone in your company who uses email and possibly (depending on your company's policy) the names and addresses of people outside the company who you can access through Notes Mail. As company personnel changes, your administrator updates the information. You, however, cannot make entries in this book, although you can update your personal information.

TIP   **No Public Address Book Icon?**   If you're a remote user, you might not see the Public Address Book icon. You can add it to your workspace, as described in Lesson 24.

In addition to the employees listed in the Public Address Book, there might also be listings for people that your company contacts frequently via another Notes server or the Internet—vendors, customers, information sources, or servers in other locations. If someone is listed in the Public Address Book, you should be able to send mail to him or her, no matter where he or she is located.

To see the names listed in your Public Address Book, double-click the Public Address Book icon. In the navigator pane (see Figure 9.2), click **People** to see a list of the people in the address book. To learn more information about an individual, double-click on that person's name. Press **Esc** to exit the person's document.

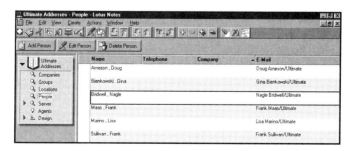

FIGURE 9.2   The Public Address Book.

USING YOUR PERSONAL ADDRESS BOOK

The Personal Address Book is where you store the names and addresses of the people to whom you send email but are not included in the Public Address Book. Because everyone in your company is already in the Public Address Book, entries in your Personal Address Book are for people to whom you want to send mail through the Internet or people who work for another company whose Lotus Notes server exchanges mail with your Lotus Notes server. Only remote users need to add people from the Public Address Book to their Personal Address Book because they only have one address book when they're not connected to the network.

To open your Personal Address Book, double-click the database icon. The navigator displays the following views:

- **Business Cards**   Lists all the people you have in your Personal Address Book, their telephone numbers, and their company names. (If you are new to Lotus Notes Mail, your address book is probably empty.)

- **By Category**   Lists all the people in your Personal Address Book, sorted into categories that you create.

- **Groups**   Lists the groups of people you created as mailing distribution lists.

- **Advanced**   When expanded, shows the Certificates, Connections, and Locations views.

- **Agents**   Like macros, agents automate Notes applications. Agents are beyond the scope of this book.

- **Design**   Contains views needed for designing applications. Design is beyond the scope of this book. You might not see this view listed if you haven't been granted design access.

CREATING BUSINESS CARDS

The information you store about a person— email address, company, and so on—appears in a Business Card document, such as the one shown in Figure 9.3.

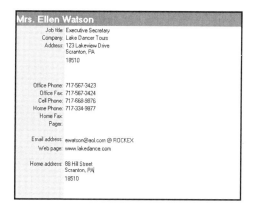

FIGURE 9.3   A Business Card document.

To create a Business Card document for a new person, follow these steps:

1. Double-click your Personal Address Book icon on the workspace.

2. Click the **Business Cards** view in the navigator pane.

3. Click the **Add Card** button on the Action bar or choose **Create**, **Business Card** from the menu. The Business Card form appears (refer to Figure 9.3).

4. Complete each field in the Business Card form by clicking within the square brackets and typing the appropriate information. Use the **Tab** key or the mouse to move from field to field.

   In some fields, such as Name, Company, Address, Office Phone, E-mail Address, and Home Address, click the small down arrow next to the field to open a dialog box that helps you fill in the details of that field (see Figure 9.4).

FIGURE 9.4   The Name Fields dialog box helps you enter information in the Name field.

5. When you click the down arrow key next to the E-mail Address field, the Mail Address Assistant dialog box appears (see Figure 9.5). In this dialog box, enter the type of mail system that person uses (Fax, Internet Mail, Lotus cc:Mail, Lotus Notes, X 400 Mail, or Other). If you aren't sure which mail system to choose, consult your Notes system administrator. Click **OK**.

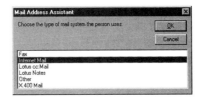

FIGURE 9.5   Choose the person's mail system from the Mail Address Assistant dialog box.

6. A second Mail Address Assistant dialog box appears, enabling you to fill in the name and the address, or domain, of that user (see Figure 9.6). Consult your Notes administrator if you're not sure how to enter the address, especially for Internet and Fax addresses. Fill in this information, and click **OK**.

What's a Domain?   A *domain* is a group of servers listed in one Public Address Book. If you don't know the domain name, see your Notes administrator. For more information on Internet Mail, see Lesson 25.

FIGURE 9.6   Enter the email address and/or domain.

7. Complete the Categories field. In the By Category view, the business cards are sorted, based on the label you enter in this field. Be consistent and watch your spelling, or you'll end up with several similar categories—Friends, Friend, Fiend—which makes it harder to find people.

8. Fill in the information for the remaining fields of the document. These fields are not mandatory, but this is a useful central storage place for information and turns your Personal Address Book into a contact management database.

TIP   **Visit Web Sites**   If you enter the address of a company web site in the Web Page field, you can visit that web page directly from the Personal Address Book (provided you have access to the Internet from your computer). In the Business Cards or By Category view, select the name of the person and then click the Visit Web Page button on the Action bar.

9. Click the **Save and Close** button on the Action bar to save this information in your address book.

TIP   **Adding a Person from a Mail Message**   When you receive a mail message from a person who is not listed in your Personal Address Book, you can add them. Open or select the mail message and then choose **Actions**, **Mail Tools**, **Add Sender to Address Book** from the menu.

CREATING AND USING GROUPS

If you want to send a mail message to more than one person, you can type each person's name, separated by a comma, or you can create a *Group*. To create a group, follow these steps:

1. Open your Personal Address Book.

2. In the navigator pane, select **Groups**.

3. Click the **Add Group** button on the Action bar.

4. The Group form appears (see Figure 9.7). Type a name for your group in the **Group Name** field. Make the group name descriptive but short enough to type easily.

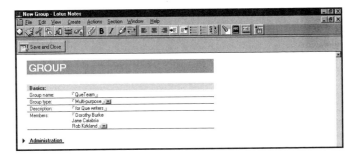

FIGURE 9.7   A group document.

5. To fill out the **Group Type** field, click the down arrow next to the field to see a list of group types, and choose one of the following:

   • **Multipurpose**   Enables you to use this list for purposes other than mail.

   • **Access Control List Only**   Only used to specify security levels in Access Control Lists. Used by the Notes administrator and not relevant to the Personal Address Book.

- **Mail Only**   Used to define mailing lists. This is the selection you choose for groups. When you choose this option, the Group document becomes a Mailing List document.

- **Deny List Only**   Only used by the Notes administrator. Not applicable to the Personal Address Book.

6. Type a short description of the group in the Description field. Although this is not a mandatory field, it might remind you why you created this group.

7. Type the names of the members in the Members field, separating the names with commas. Or, click the down arrow next to the field and select the names from your Personal Address Book.

8. When you're done, click the **Save and Close** button.

9. Close the address book by pressing your Esc key.

Mailing Lists   If you intend the group to be used only as a mail distribution list, click the **Add Mailing List** button on the Action bar when you want to create the group. Mail Only is entered automatically in the Group Type field.

Creating Groups from Other Documents   If you have a mail message, meeting invitation, or task document open that includes a list of recipients, you can create a group for that list. Choose **Actions**, **Copy Into**, **New Group** from the menu. A new group document opens with the Members field filled in with the names in the list. Complete the other fields and save the document.

After you create the group, you can use it when you address memos. Simply type the name of the group in the To field (Quick address completes the name as you type), and Notes sends your email to all the people in the group. If a person drops out of the group or a new person is added, you can edit the group document by selecting it from the Groups view and clicking the **Edit Group** button on the Action bar. By using the group name when addressing your mail, you can save a lot of typing.

TIP **Too Much Mail?**   Lotus Notes saves a copy of your mail by default. Including yourself in a group results in your having two copies of a mail message, the one you saved and the one you received as a member of the group.

Some groups need to exist only for the length of a project on which you're working. When you need to remove a group from your Personal Address Book, select it from the Groups view and click the **Delete Group** button on the Action bar.

CREATING A MAIL MESSAGE FROM THE PERSONAL ADDRESS BOOK

When you have the Personal Address Book open, you can create a mail message without having to switch to your mail database. Follow these steps:

1. Display the Business Cards or By Category view.

2. Select the names of the people to whom you want to send your message (to select more than one person, click in the margin in front of each name to place a check mark there).

3. Click the **Write Memo** button on the Action bar.

4. A new mail memo opens with the selected names in the To field. Fill in any names you need in the cc and bcc fields and add a subject. Type your message in the body field and then click **Send**.

In this lesson, you learned about the two address books, how to create Business Cards for people to whom you want to address mail, how to set up mailing lists, and how to send mail directly from the Personal Address Book. In the next lesson, you will learn more about sending mail messages.

Sending Mail Messages

10

In this lesson, you learn how to apply mail delivery options and how to set send options.

Using Delivery Options

Before you send your mail, you can set several delivery options to do the following:

- Let recipients know your message is important
- Place a digital signature on your message
- Encrypt your message
- Set delivery priorities
- Request confirmation that the message was received
- Request confirmation that the message was read
- Prevent addressees from copying the message

Encrypt Sounds like you need to put on your magic decoder ring! When you choose to encrypt a message, Lotus Notes scrambles the message, and only the recipient has the key to unscramble it. Because your message travels from your PC to the Lotus Notes server and then to the PC of the recipient, encrypting the message prevents anyone who might be working at the Lotus Notes server from reading your message.

To set delivery options, click the **Delivery Options** button on the action bar. The Delivery Options dialog box appears (see Figure 10.1).

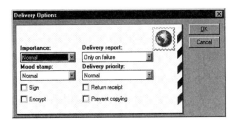

FIGURE 10.1   The Delivery Options dialog box.

Setting Importance lets the recipient know how important your message is. Choose **Normal, High,** or **Low** in the Importance drop-down list. If you choose High, the recipient see a red exclamation mark **!** next to your mail message in her Inbox (see Figure 10.2). Choosing Normal or Low does not affect how your mail message appears in the recipient's Inbox at all.

!	Jane Calabria	07/02/97	⬩	One more Appendix - AR for works
!	Jane Calabria	07/02/97		pushing a hi priority
!	Jane Calabria	07/02/97		Take this!

FIGURE 10.2   The High Importance indicator.

To add a digital signature, which lets the recipient know you are the person who created the message, choose **Sign** in the Delivery Options dialog box.

To encrypt your mail, select **Encrypt** in the Delivery Options dialog box. Note, however, that your recipient must exist in the Public Address Book, as encryption is accomplished by using a number called the public key that is stored in each Person Document in the Public Address Book.

DELIVERY PRIORITY

The Delivery Priority determines how the Lotus Notes server handles your mail when it receives your message on its way to the recipient.

Delivery Priority affects mail that crosses servers only, such as mail that is sent to a recipient via the Internet or other Lotus Notes servers. It can override the regularly scheduled time that servers call to exchange mail. If your mail is urgent, setting the Delivery Priority to High forces your server to immediately call another server and deliver your mail. This is very useful if you have an urgent message. If you set the Delivery Priority to Normal (the default value), your mail travels across servers at the predetermined time(s) set by your Lotus Notes administrator. If you set the Delivery Priority to Low, your mail is sent between the hours of 2 A.M. and 6 A.M., the default time for low priority, unless your Notes administrator has changed that time. This is a good option if you're sending large attachments (as discussed in Lesson 14). Using a Low priority sends this mail during off-peak hours.

DELIVERY REPORT

The delivery report (see Figure 10.3) provides different information about the delivery of your message to the recipient:

- **Only on Failure** (the default value)   Returns a delivery failure report to you if your mail can't be delivered.

- **Confirm Delivery**   Returns a confirmation notice indicating that your mail delivery was successful. If you ask for a confirm delivery report for each mail message you sent, your Inbox will be full of notices! Use this choice sparingly.

- **Trace Entire Path**   Returns a report telling you the path your mail took to get to its recipient. If you are having problems with your mail, your Lotus Notes administrator might ask you to use this option to determine the source of the problem.

- **None**   Mutes the delivery report. You'll get no delivery reports at all—even if your mail could not be delivered to the recipient.

Simply because a person has *received* your mail doesn't mean that she has *read* it. Selecting **Return Receipt** in the Delivery Options dialog box notifies you that the recipient has read your message. This works only for other Lotus Notes Mail users, not across the Internet.

Mail Router	09/28/97	📎 DELIVERY FAILURE: User kpurdom not listed in public Name & Address Book

FIGURE 10.3   The delivery failure report.

PREVENT COPYING

The Prevent Copying option in the Delivery Options dialog box restricts what happens to your message after other Notes users receive it. You can prevent the recipient from copying the message to the Windows Clipboard, forwarding the message to another person, creating a reply with history (as described in Lesson 12), or printing your message. Again, this only applies to other Notes Mail users.

After you have chosen your delivery options, click **OK** to apply them to your message.

CREATING MOOD STAMPS

Pay special attention to the Mood Stamps option on the Delivery Options dialog box. You can use mood stamps to tell your recipients what type of mood your message holds. When they view the Inbox, they'll see icons to the left of your mail message, indicating your mail message "mood" (see Figure 10.4). Notes creates these icons for all moods except Normal.

Who	▲ Date ▼	Subject
🕐 Winny Gold	09/12/96	Dinner after the meeting?
Thomas Moran	09/12/96	Interview for new assistant Tuesday
★ Thomas Moran	09/12/96	Excellence Awards Announced at TOYEXPO
📁 Tina Farnet	09/12/96	WW Holiday Schedule
✓ Thomas Moran	09/12/96	Clean up old discussion database
! Tina Farnet	09/12/96	Deadline for TAC presentation is now tomorrow
♦ Thomas Moran	09/12/96	I really needed your help yesterday
📖 Tina Farnet	09/12/96	Need Supplier's Catalog
📖 Thomas Moran	09/12/96	I need the PO for Magical Mysteries
Ralph Martin	09/12/96	Fran King of King Education
🕐 Ralph Martin	09/12/96	Do you know the order number fo Nature Toys?
Ralph Martin	09/12/96	Phone Message from JJ Smith
Thomas Moran	09/12/96	RECEIVED: Tomorrow's fine for lunch
🕐 Randy Neusam	09/12/96	Have you spoken to Theo Frank?
📁 Randy Neusam	09/12/96	Info on LearnComm's History Products
! Winny Gold	09/12/96	Mickey Server is DOWN - can't get proposall

FIGURE 10.4   Mood stamp displays in the Inbox.

To attach a mood stamp to your mail message, click the **Delivery Options** button on the Action bar. In the Delivery Options dialog box, select a message type from the Mood Stamp drop-down list: Normal, Personal, Confidential, Private, Thank You, Flame (this means you're truly angry at someone), Good Job!, Joke, FYI, Question, or Reminder. Then, click **OK**.

Why Is He Mad at Me?   Lots of new Notes users think that the Flame mood stamp indicates that a message is "hot" or important. In the true Net Etiquette sense, flaming is insulting (see Lesson 6). You might want to think twice about using this icon.

SETTING SEND OPTIONS

You can find less frequently used mail options by choosing **Actions**, **Special Options** from the menu. From the Special Options dialog box, you can set options to automatically delete mail messages from your Mail database, archive messages, and request a reply by a specific date (see Figure 10.5).

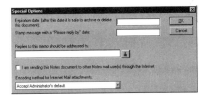

FIGURE 10.5   The Special Options dialog box.

If you want to automatically delete or archive your memo, type a date in the Expiration Date field of the Special Options dialog box. Archiving is discussed in Lesson 13.

To request a response to your mail message by a certain date, you can enter a date in the Stamp Message With a "Please Reply By" Date box. That request will be sent as part of the mail message.

If you want the response to your mail to be sent to someone else (not you), you can indicate that information by filling out the Replies to This Memo Should Be Addressed to box. For example, if you type **Mary Jane Kane** in this box, you see a note at the top of your memo that says **Please respond to Mary Jane Kane**.

Your Lotus Notes mail message appears as plain text when someone on the Internet receives. That's just the way it works; formatting options don't always interpret well. But if you send mail to another Lotus Notes Mail user through the Internet, he can see your text formatting if you select the **I am Sending This Notes Document to Other Notes Mail User(s) Through the Internet** option. Making this selection doesn't guarantee the transfer of formatting options, because your message might travel through many different servers. But failing to select this option guarantees that the Lotus Notes Mail formatting options will be lost—regardless of the product used by the recipient.

To close the Special Options dialog box, click **OK**.

SAVING COPIES

To send and file your mail at the same time, click the **Send and File** button on the Action bar. With this option, Notes files your sent copy in the folder you specify, as opposed to your Sent folder. When you choose **Send and File**, the Move to Folder dialog box appears, listing your available folders. Select the folder you want to use.

To remove a document from a folder without deleting it from the database, choose **Actions**, **Remove from Folder**.

Some companies restrict the sizes of mail databases. If your company is concerned with space, you might want to disable the **Always Keep a Copy** option of user preferences and have Notes prompt you with an option to save a copy every time you send a new message.

In this lesson, you learned how to use delivery options and how to set send options for mail. You also learned how to file a copy of your mail message at the time you send it. In the next lesson, you will learn about reading mail you receive.

11 READING AND PRINTING MAIL

In this lesson, you learn how to use the Preview pane and change views while reading your mail. You also learn about read marks and printing.

OPENING YOUR MAIL

You can access mail from the workspace, from the opened mail database, and from your status bar. Mail is an important part of the Notes program and accessing and reading mail is an easy process.

> **TIP** **No Mail?** If you're new to Lotus Notes Mail, you might not have mail in your Inbox. In preparation for this lesson, call your coworkers and ask them to send you mail so you have mail in your Inbox to work with during this lesson (or send some mail to yourself).

To access your incoming mail, you have three options:

- From the workspace, double-click the mail database icon. When the database opens (by default, at your Inbox view), double-click the piece of mail you want to read.

- Click the Inbox (or Mail) icon located on the bottom right of the status bar. Select **Scan Unread Mail** to open the first unread mail message in your Inbox.

- From the workspace, select the mail database. Choose **Edit**, **Unread Marks**, **Scan Unread** to open the first unread mail message in the Inbox.

When you finish reading your mail message, you can press the **Esc** key to return to your Inbox, or you can continue to read un-opened (unread) messages by using the SmartIcons. After you open a mail message, there are four SmartIcons to assist you in navigating through your mail, without the need to return to the Inbox:

Use the **Navigate Next** and **Navigate Previous** SmartIcons (plain up and down arrow icons) to navigate to the next or the previous mail message.

The **Navigate Next Unread** and **Navigate Previous Unread** SmartIcons (up and down arrow icons with stars) take you to the next or the previous unread message.

When you finish reading your mail, press **Esc** to return to your Inbox.

> **TIP** **Adding a Sender** The easiest way to add a person to your address book is while you're reading his mail message. Choose **Actions**, **Mail Tools**, **Add Sender to Address Book** from the menu. A confirmation box appears. Click **OK**. For more information about Notes Mail address books, see Lesson 9.

UNDERSTANDING READ MARKS

When you see your messages listed in the Inbox, you can tell at a glance which messages you've read. Mail messages you haven't read appear in red with a star to the left of the mail message. After you open and read the message, the star disappears and the mail message appears in black in your Inbox. Figure 11.1 shows read and unread mail messages in the Inbox.

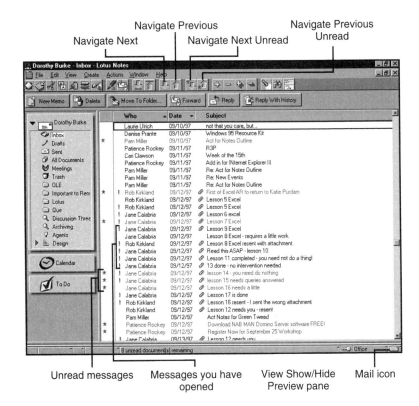

Navigate Next

Navigate Previous

Navigate Next Unread

Navigate Previous Unread

Unread messages   Messages you have   View Show/Hide   Mail icon
                    opened   Preview pane

FIGURE 11.1   Read marks displayed in Inbox.

If you have a large number of unread messages, and you don't
want to open each one to remove the unread marks, you can
change the unread marks to read by choosing **Edit**, **Unread
Marks**, **Mark All Read**.

Notes can display the number of unread documents contained in
a database by displaying the number on the database icon (see
Figure 11.2). When you're at the workspace, choose **View**, **Show
Unread** from the menu. A small box appears on each database
icon, showing the number of unread documents and telling you,
without opening your mail database, that you have unread mail
messages.

FIGURE 11.2   The number of unread documents displayed on icon.

CHANGING VIEWS

As you learned in Lesson 4, there are several ways to view your mail. You can sort how mail appears in your Inbox by using the sorting icons located on the column headers of the Who and the Date columns. By default, the Inbox is sorted by date with the most current date at the bottom of your screen. So, new mail appears at the bottom of the list. If you want new mail to appear at the top of the list, click the triangle located in the header of the Date column.

If you click the triangle located in the Who column, the triangle turns blue, and your mail sorts alphabetically by the first name of the sender. This is useful when you need to find a mail message sent by a particular person, and you don't remember the date or the subject. Just be aware that this view is ordered by *first* name.

When the column isn't wide enough to display the information, you can widen it by pointing at the separator line between the column headings and then dragging it to the right. The column widths return to their original settings the next time you open that view.

To have only unread mail show in your Inbox, choose **View**, **Show**, **Unread Only** from the menu. Now, only unread mail messages appear in your Inbox. You can turn on and off the option to show only unread mail at any time. You also can see all of the mail by selecting the **All Documents** view.

You also can view a list of selected documents. To select documents, click to the left of the document listing in your Inbox. A check mark appears next to that document. You can select one, many, contiguous (in order), or non-contiguous documents. After you have selected several, choose **View**, **Show**, **Selected Only** from the menu.

> **TIP** **Horizontal Scroll Bar**   If you're looking at the information in the view and you can't see the entire line, turn on the horizontal scroll bar. Choose **View, Scroll, Horizontal Scroll Bar** from the menu or just press the right arrow key.

USING THE PREVIEW PANE

You might prefer to read your mail by using the Preview pane, so you can view a mail message while viewing the Navigator pane and the list of documents in your Inbox. The Preview pane splits your Inbox into three panels. To turn on the Preview pane, choose **View**, **Document Preview** from the menu or click the **View Show/Hide Preview Pane** SmartIcon. The Document Preview pane activates (see Figure 11.3).

The Document Preview pane is adjustable. You might decide you want to see more of the message and less of the Inbox documents list. Size the Preview pane by dragging its borders.

You can use the scrollbars located in any three of these panels (the Navigator pane, the Documents pane, or the Preview pane) to scroll through the contents of each window. What displays in the Preview pane is driven by the mail message you have selected in the Documents pane. To preview mail in your Inbox, you can move through the documents located in your Inbox by doing one of the following:

- Use your up or down arrow keys on your keyboard.

- Use the **Tab** key (or **Shift+Tab** to move backward).

- Use the navigator SmartIcons located on the toolbar.

- Use your mouse to select a mail message.

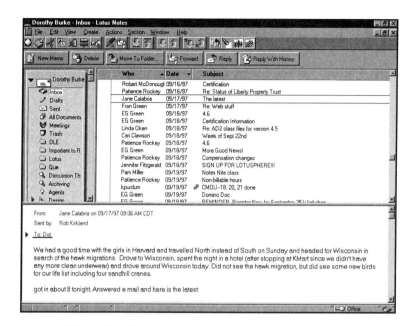

FIGURE 11.3   The Preview pane.

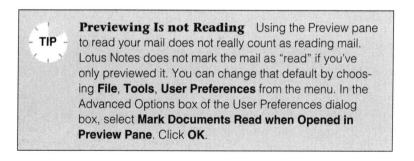

TIP **Previewing Is not Reading** Using the Preview pane to read your mail does not really count as reading mail. Lotus Notes does not mark the mail as "read" if you've only previewed it. You can change that default by choosing **File**, **Tools**, **User Preferences** from the menu. In the Advanced Options box of the User Preferences dialog box, select **Mark Documents Read when Opened in Preview Pane**. Click **OK**.

You can configure the Preview pane to look differently than the three-panel split. Choose **View**, **Arrange Preview** to see the Preview Pane dialog box for your options (see Figure 11.4).

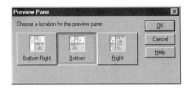

FIGURE 11.4   The Preview Pane dialog box.

The default selection is Bottom, which refers to the position of the Preview pane. You can select Bottom Right or Right, and you also can resize these panels after you make your selection.

PRINTING MAIL

You can print one or several pieces of mail at a time. As with many Windows products, you can activate the Print command in several ways. In Lesson 3, you added the Print SmartIcon to your toolbar; using the Print icon is one way to print a single copy of mail. To print more than one mail message at a time, select those messages by clicking next to each one in the left column of the Inbox view. This places a check mark next to the mail message. Then, print by using one of the following methods:

- Click the **Print** SmartIcon once. This prints one copy of the open mail message.

- Hold down the **Ctrl** key while pressing the letter **p**. This also prints one copy of the open mail message.

- Select **File**, **Print** from the menu. This gives you the option to print multiple copies, headers, and footer, change the orientation of the printer, or change the printer selection.

If you want to print more than one copy of your mail, choose **File**, **Print** from the menu. In the File Print dialog box (see Figure 11.5), indicate the number of copies you want to print in the Copies box. Click **OK** to print the copies.

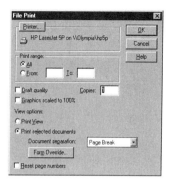

FIGURE 11.5   The File Print dialog box.

It might be useful, at times, to print a view. To print a view, choose **File**, **Print** from the menu. In the View Options portion of the Print dialog box, click **Print View**. Click **OK** to print.

To print more than one mail message from the view, select the documents you want to print by clicking the margin before each one to place a check mark there. Then, choose **File**, **Print** from the menu. In the **View Options** portion of the Print dialog box, click **Print Selected Documents**. Click **OK**.

In this lesson, you learned how to work with Read Marks and set your preferences for scanning unread documents. You also learned about various views and previewing mail. You also learned how to print your mail. In the next lesson, you will learn how to reply to mail.

12 REPLYING TO MAIL

In this lesson, you learn about options for replying to mail. You also learn how to add people to your address book.

UNDERSTANDING REPLIES

Often, you must respond to mail messages. Responding to mail is similar to creating a new mail message because you use the same form. When you reply to mail, however, you do have different options than when you create mail. For example, you can include the original mail message in your reply message. (When you reply to a mail message, remember the email etiquette covered in Lesson 6.)

USING REPLY OPTIONS

There are two buttons for replying to mail on the Action bar of your Inbox: **Reply** and **Reply With History**. To see these buttons, double-click the mail database icon in your workspace; the mail Inbox opens. Double-click the mail message to which you want to reply. The mail message appears, similar to the one shown in Figure 12.1.

A third option, Reply To All, which appears after you have selected one of the previous actions, enables you to reply to all the recipients of the original mail message. You learn how to use all three reply options in the following sections.

Reply button   Reply with History button

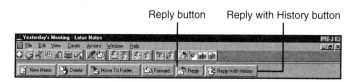

FIGURE 12.1   A mail message that requires a reply.

REPLY

To respond to a message by using the Reply option, do the following:

1. Click the **Reply** button located on the Action bar. A new mail message appears in which to write your reply (see Figure 12.2). The To field and the Subject line already contain the recipient's name and the subject of the previous message.

2. Fill in the body of the mail message; then, click the **Send** button located on the Action bar to send the message.

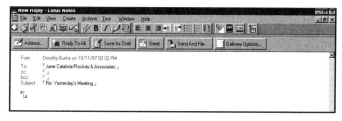

FIGURE 12.2   Replying to a mail message.

It might be helpful to see the original message on your screen while typing your reply. To view the original message while typing a response, choose **View**, **Parent Preview** from the menu.

REPLY WITH HISTORY

There is another way to reply to a piece of mail. You can avoid a lot of typing by answering questions with words such as "yes" and "no." If you respond this way, however, the person receiving your reply might not understand to which questions you're responding.

To keep your typing to a minimum and to help the original sender remember what this message was about, you can select **Reply With History** on the Action bar to send your response back with the original message that was sent to you. Figure 12.3 shows the result of this option. You can complete the reply form, and the original memo is sent along with your reply.

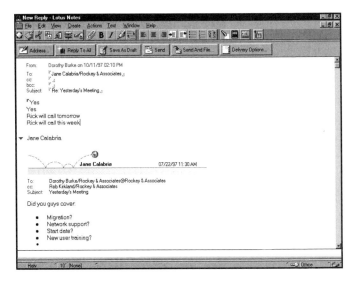

FIGURE 12.3   Using the Reply With History option.

After you complete the Reply With History, click the **Send** button located on the Action bar to send this message.

REPLY TO ALL

The third reply option, Reply To All, does not appear on the Action bar where you find Reply and Reply With History. Instead, the Reply To All option appears on the action bar *after* you select **Reply** or **Reply With History**. For example, say that Jane sends a mail message to Dorothy and includes Rob in the cc field. Obviously, Jane wants Rob to know that she is asking Dorothy for information. When Dorothy chooses the Reply With History option, only Jane's name (the sender) appears on the mail memo. Dorothy then chooses Reply To All as her reply option to include Rob in the reply. His name appears in the field in which the sender originally included it, in this case, the cc field.

When the new mail message appears ready for a reply, the Action bar includes a Reply To All button. Click the **Reply To All** button to include the original recipients of this message. Figure 12.4 shows the results of choosing the Reply To All option after the New Reply form is onscreen.

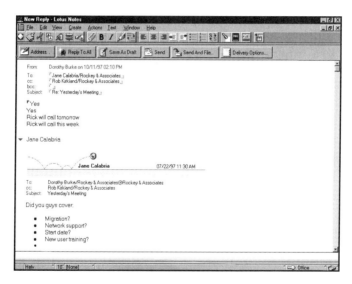

FIGURE 12.4   Selecting Reply To All fills in the names of the recipients of the original mail message.

> **Forget Reply To All?**   It's easy to forget to use the Reply To All option because it does not appear on the first Action bar while reading mail. If you send your reply without using Reply To All, you can re-create your reply by using Reply To All, or you can forward your saved copy to the others in the original distribution list. You learn about forwarding later in this lesson.

FORWARDING MAIL

You might receive a mail message that you want to forward to someone else. To forward a mail message, open the message and click the **Forward** button on the Action bar. Fill in the address portion of the message and include any message you want to send along with the original. Send the mail as you would any other piece of mail (see Figure 12.5).

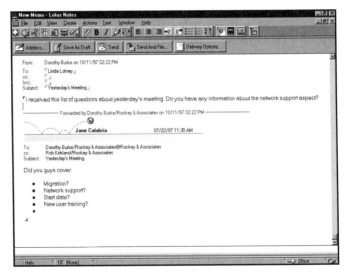

FIGURE 12.5   A forwarded message.

In this lesson, you learned about the options for replying to mail. In the next lesson, you will learn how to delete mail and use folders.

MANAGING MAIL MESSAGES

13

*In this lesson, you learn about deleting
mail messages, creating folders, using the Discussion Thread view,
archiving old mail, and viewing sent mail.*

DELETING MAIL

To keep your Mail database manageable, make it a practice to
clear out old messages periodically. If you're not sure if you'll
need the message again, archive it. If you know you won't need
the message any longer, delete it.

In Lotus Notes, deleting messages is a two-step process. First, mark
the message for deletion; then, remove it by emptying the Trash.

You can mark messages for deletion while you're reading them, or
you can do it from the View pane. To delete a message while you
are in read mode, do the following:

1. In the opened message, click the **Delete** button on the
   Action bar or press the **Delete** key on your keyboard.

2. Lotus Notes marks that message for deletion, and your
   next message appears.

You Didn't Mean to Click the Delete Button So far,
you've only marked the message for deletion. If you didn't
mean to do this, and the trash can appears next to the
document in the view, just press **Delete** again; otherwise,
open the Trash folder, select the message, and press the
Delete key to remove the mark.

3. Continue reading the rest of your messages, deleting those you don't want to keep.

To mark messages for deletion while you are in the View pane (or Inbox), you must first select the message or messages you want to delete by using one of the following methods:

- Select a single message to delete by pressing delete with the message selected in the view.

- If you want to select several messages in a row, click the first message and drag up or down the left side of the messages. This places a check mark next to all of the messages you drag past. You also can select messages that are not next to each other, by clicking to the left side of each of the messages to place check marks in the margin.

- Choose **Edit**, **Select All** to select all of the messages in the view.

If you accidentally select a document you don't want to mark, click the check mark to remove it. To remove all the check marks, choose **Edit**, **Deselect All**.

To mark the selected documents for deletion, press the **Delete** key or click the **Delete** button on the Action bar. A trash can appears next to each item you mark for deletion. When you exit the database, you might be prompted with a message, asking if you want to permanently delete these messages. Click **Yes**.

CREATING FOLDERS

When you frequently use email at work, you'll receive many messages. You might not want to delete every mail message, and it's not practical to save everything in your Inbox, but you can organize your work by creating folders to store your mail messages. You can create whatever folders you need and then put the appropriate messages into the folders, much like organizing a file cabinet. To create a folder, do the following:

1. Choose **Create**, **Folder** from the menu bar.

2. In the Create Folder dialog box, enter a name in the
   Folder name box (see Figure 13.1).

FIGURE 13.1   The Create Folder dialog box.

3. If you want to put the new folder inside an existing one
   (like putting a manila folder inside a Pendaflex® folder in
   a filing cabinet), click that folder from the **Select a Location for the New Folder** list box.

4. Click **OK**.

To place mail messages in the folder, you can

- Drag them

- Use the menu commands

- Use the action bar

To drag documents to folders from your Inbox, do the following:

1. Select the document (or documents) you want to move
   into the folder.

2. Click the document and drag it until it is over the folder.

3. When the mouse pointer is over the folder, it changes to
   a small document icon with a plus (+) sign over it. Release
   the mouse button.

Dragging a mail message moves the message to a folder, removing it from the current folder (in this case, your Inbox). If you hold down the **Ctrl** key while dragging, you can add the message to a different folder, leaving a copy of it in its current folder.

Documents or Messages?   In Lesson 1, you learned that everything in a Lotus Notes database is stored in a document. Mail messages are no exception. Technically, we call them documents. In email terms, we call them messages.

Other ways to move mail messages are to use the menu commands. To move a mail message to another folder by using the menu, do the following:

1. If you're in the Inbox, select the document(s) you want to put in a folder (if you're reading the message, only that document moves to the folder).

2. Choose **Actions**, **Move to Folder** or click the **Move to Folder** button on the Action bar.

3. In the Move To Folder dialog box (see Figure 13.2), click a folder name in the **Select a Folder** list box (click the **Create New Folder** button if you haven't made the folder yet).

FIGURE 13.2   The Move To Folder dialog box.

4. Click the **Add** button to put the mail message into the folder without removing it from other folders. Click the

Move button to put the mail message into the folder while removing it from other folders (you cannot remove the message from a view).

Deleting from Folders Be careful deleting documents from your folders, because this action deletes the document from your mail database. When you place a document in a folder or folders, it does not make a new copy of the document for each location; you are actually creating a pointer to that one document in the database. If you no longer want a particular document in a folder, select it and choose **Actions, Remove from Folder**.

DISCUSSION THREAD VIEW

Mail messages frequently turn into conversations; for instance: Joe sends a message to Mary, Tim, and Jack inquiring about their vacation plans. Mary replies that she is going to Cape Cod for a week in August. Joe replies to Mary that he knows a great place for dinner on the Cape. Meanwhile, Tim responds to Joe's original message, as does Jack. A conversation is born.

Messages that are responses to previous memos have a Document Link icon and a Re: at the beginning of the subject line (see Figure 13.3). If you want to review the message being replied to, double-click the icon to open that document. You'll learn how to make your own document links in Lesson 15.

If you have a long conversation, the best way to follow it from beginning to end is to look in the Discussion Thread view. Click the **Discussion Thread View** icon in the navigator pane to see the list of documents organized by conversations (see Figure 13.4). The subject line of reply messages appears indented, and replies to replies appear further indented.

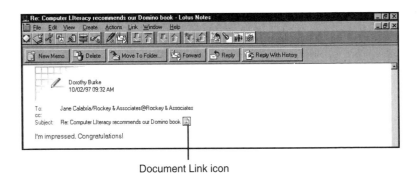

Document Link icon

FIGURE 13.3 A reply to a message.

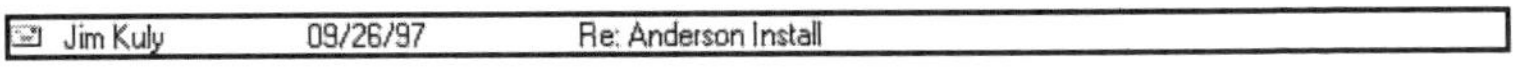

| Jim Kuly | 09/26/97 | Re: Anderson Install |

FIGURE 13.4 The Discussion Thread view.

ARCHIVING MAIL

There are several strategies for reducing the size of your mail database, and archiving old mail messages is one of them. Archiving stores the old messages in another database, making your mail database more manageable. You can have these messages archived automatically or do it manually.

To set up automatic archiving, do the following:

1. In the Navigator pane, double-click the **Archiving** view icon to open that view.

2. Click the **Setup Archive** button on the Action bar (see Figure 13.5).

3. The Archive Profile form appears, as shown in Figure 13.6. Complete the Archive Profile form. You can fill in any of the following options:

> Check **Archive Expired Documents** and set the number of days before a document is archived.

Check **Archive Documents Which Have No Activity** and set a time limit (in days).

Check whether you want to **Generate an Archive Log Each Time an Archive Occurs**.

Check **Include Document Links** if you want to add them to the archive.

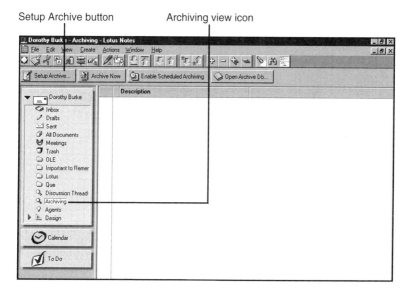

FIGURE **13.5**   The Archiving view.

4. Choose whether or not the documents will be archived Locally (on your PC) or On Server by clicking the **Specify Archive Location** button on the Action bar and selecting the appropriate option from the **Documents Are Archived** box in the Lotus Notes dialog box. You must be allowed to create databases on the server to create the Archive database there. You might not have this capability.

Specify Archive
Location button

Select location and name
of archive database

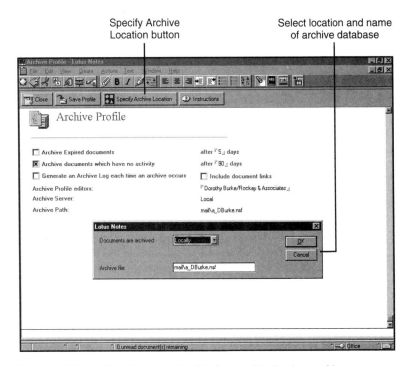

FIGURE 13.6   The Archive Profile form with the Lotus Notes
dialog box open.

5. You can enter the name of the database file (if you don't
   want to use the one that Lotus Notes generates automatically) in the Archive File box. Click **OK** to return to the
   Archive Profile document.

6. Click the **Save Profile** button on the Action bar.

7. When the dialog box appears saying that the Archive
   database has been created, click **OK**.

8. Click the **Close** button on the Action bar.

9. Switch temporarily to another folder or view in your Mail database and then back to the Archiving view.

10. Click the **Enable Scheduling Archiving** button on the Action bar to activate the automatic archiving.

If you decide to turn off automatic archiving, open the Archiving view and click the **Disable Scheduled Archiving** button on the Action bar.

You don't have to wait for Lotus Notes to archive your messages based on the schedule you set up. Select the messages that you want to archive and choose **Actions**, **Mail Tools**, **Archive Selected Documents**.

After you have documents in the Archive database, you can view them by opening the database. From the Archiving view, click the **Open Archive Db** button on the Action bar. Then, open the messages you want to read.

If you set up an Archive Log in your Archive Profile document and chose to include document links, you also can view the archived messages by opening the Log (see Figure 13.7). From the Archiving view, open the Archive Log that has the message you want to see. Click the Link icon, read the message, and then close it.

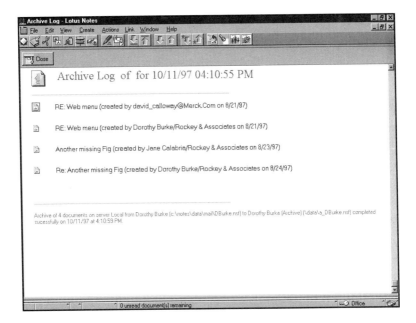

FIGURE 13.7   An Archive Log.

In this lesson, you learned about managing your mail messages by deleting or archiving old messages, viewing conversations in the Discussion Thread view, seeing the messages you sent in the Sent folder, and creating your own folders. In the next lesson, you will learn about attaching non-Notes files to your messages.

ATTACHING FILES

In this lesson, you learn how to create, manage, detach, and launch file attachments.

UNDERSTANDING ATTACHMENTS

There might be times when you want to send a file to someone through email. That file might be a Lotus Notes database, a spreadsheet, a word processing document, a compressed file, a graphic file, or a scanned photograph of your grandchildren—almost any type of file. In Lotus Notes, you can attach an entire file within the rich text field, or body, of your mail message and send it. The file you attach is a copy, so your original remains intact on your computer.

The user who receives your mail can detach your file and save it. If the recipient has the same application program in which the file was created, she can launch the application, opening the file in its native application.

Attachments can be placed only in rich text fields, and the body of the mail message (where you type your message) is the only rich text field in the Mail Message form.

CREATING ATTACHMENTS

To attach a file to a Lotus Notes mail message, do the following:

1. Create the mail message. Make sure your insertion point (cursor) is in the message body at the exact point at which you want the attachment to appear.

2. Choose **File**, **Attach** or click the **File Attach** SmartIcon. The Create Attachment(s) dialog box appears, as shown in Figure 14.1.

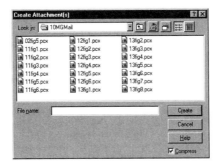

FIGURE 14.1   The Create Attachment(s) dialog box.

3. In the Create Attachment(s) dialog box, enter the name of the file you want to attach in the **File Name** box and then specify its location by choosing the correct drive and directory, or folder. Or, specify the location first and then select the filename from the list.

4. The compress file box is enabled by default. Leave this box checked.

TIP   **Compressed Files**   Compressed files transfer faster than those that are not compressed. It might take a little longer to attach the file to your message, however, because Notes compresses the file during the attachment process. A compressed file also takes up less disk space on the server.

5. Click the **Create** button. The attached file appears as an icon within the body of your mail message.

The appearance of the icon depends on the type of file it represents and whether or not you have the original software that this file was created in installed on your PC. If you are attaching a Lotus 1-2-3 file, you see a Lotus 1-2-3 icon in your mail message. If the file is a Microsoft Word file, you see a Microsoft Word icon in your mail message. If you don't have native software installed for that file, you see a generic document icon.

When you receive mail that has an attachment, a paper clip icon appears next to the mail message in your Inbox (see Figure 14.2).

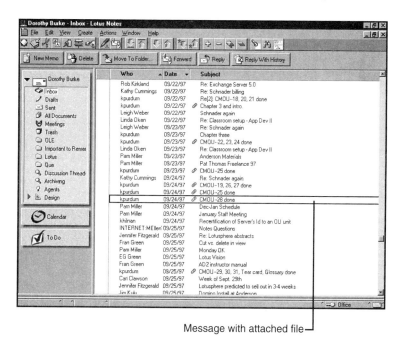

Message with attached file

FIGURE 14.2   A paper clip icon in the Inbox indicates an attachment.

VIEWING ATTACHMENTS

When you receive an attached file, you can view the file to see what it is, even if you don't have the application that runs it.

Open the mail message, double-click the attachment icon, and
click the **View** button in the Properties box (see Figure 14.3). Be
aware that when you view the file this way, the files you see are
unformatted; they're straight text only. After you finish looking at
the file, press **Esc** to leave the view.

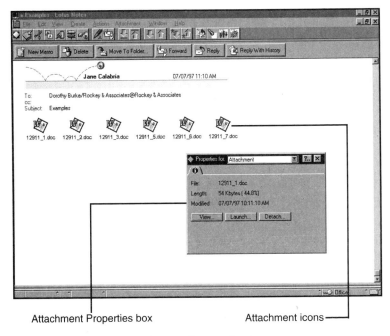

Attachment Properties box   Attachment icons

FIGURE 14.3   The Attachment Properties box.

Can't View an Attachment?   This problem is due to one
of three things: The Attachment Viewer wasn't installed on
your computer during the installation of Lotus Notes; the
file you're trying to view is not one that Notes supports for
viewing; you don't have the application that was used to
create the file on your hard drive or on a server to which
you're connected. Notes supports viewing of RTF, TXT,
BMP, CGM, WMF, PIC, TIFF, JPEG, GIF, EXE, ZIP, MDB,
PPT, XL*, WK*, PRE, SAM, SDW, DOC, and WPD file
formats.

The Properties box also gives you information about the attached file: its name, the size of the file, and the date and time it was last modified.

DETACHING FILES

To store the attached file on your hard disk or a network drive, detach the file. Then, at your convenience, open the file in the appropriate application. To detach a file, do the following:

1. Double-click the attached file icon.

2. Click the **Detach** button on the Properties box.

3. In the Save Attachment dialog box (see Figure 14.4), specify the filename you want to give the detached file and the drive and directory (or folder) in which you want to store it.

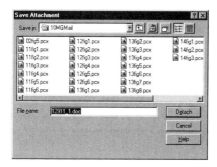

FIGURE 14.4   The Save Attachment dialog box.

4. Click the **Detach** button in the Save Attachment dialog box; close the Properties box.

To detach more than one file, select the file icons of the files you want to detach (hold down the Shift key and click each icon or drag across the icons). Then, choose **Attachments**, **Detach All Selected**; Or, to detach all the attached files, choose **Attachments**, **Detach All**. The Save Attachments To dialog box appears, as shown in Figure 14.5. Specify the drive and directory, or folder, in which you want to save the files. Click **OK**.

FIGURE 14.5 The Save Attachments to: dialog box.

LAUNCHING FILES

If you want to look at an attached file in the application in which it was created, launch the application from within mail. To launch an attachment, double-click the attachment icon and then click the **Launch** button on the Properties box. You can then view the document and make changes. You can save it or print it from the application. You can close the application when you finish with the file. Lotus Notes and your mail message remain open the entire time you are working in the other application.

Out for Launch If you can't launch the attachment, you probably don't have that application installed on your computer. A little giveaway is the icon representing the attachment. If the icon is plain and gray, there's a good chance that you don't have the application in which the attachment was originally created. You can still use the View option, as described in the beginning of this lesson, to see the unformatted contents of the attachment.

PRINTING THE ATTACHMENT

Printing the attachment is not a problem when you have the application program installed on your computer. You can print it from that program. You can still print the attachment if you don't have the application program, however, by completing the following steps:

1. Double-click the attachment icon to open the file.

2. Click the **View** button on the Properties box.

3. Choose **File**, **Print**. The Print dialog box appears (see Figure 14.6).

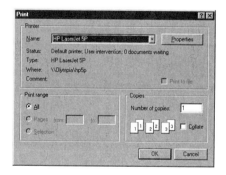

FIGURE 14.6   The Print dialog box.

4. (**Optional**) The default setting in the Print dialog box is to print all of the document. If you want to print only a portion of the attachment, highlight that segment before you choose **File**, **Print**. Then, after you open the File Print dialog box, choose **Selection** under Print Range.

5. Click **OK** to print the document.

Unexpected results, such as code lines or unusual characters, might occur when you print from the viewer. Whenever possible, therefore, it is better to print from the native application.

There is one more thing to remember when working with attachments. When you launch an attachment, Windows creates a temporary file for you to work in. If you look at the title bar of a launched attachment (no matter which application it's in), you see a series of numbers, not the original filename of the attachment sent to you. If you decide to make changes to that file and save it again, you should use the Save As command to give it a name you will remember. Also, saving changes this way does not affect the original attachment sent to you.

If you receive an attachment to which you are to make changes and then return, first detach the file. Then, open it in its original application, make your changes, save the file, and create a new mail message, attaching the modified file to return to the sender. Send the file back with a slightly modified filename, maybe with an **R** at the end of the filename so the recipient knows that you have made revisions and doesn't overwrite his original with your revised file.

In this lesson, you learned how to create, launch, detach, and print attachments. In the next lesson, you will learn how to create Lotus Notes links and pop-ups.

UNDERSTANDING LINKS AND POP-UPS

*In this lesson, you learn how to create
links within Notes to Notes documents, databases, or views. You also
learn how to create Pop-Ups.*

CREATING DOCUMENT, DATABASE, AND VIEW LINKS

Links are pointers to other documents, views, or Lotus Notes databases. If want to send a mail message and refer to a page in the Help database, you can create a document link in your mail message. When the recipient receives your mail, he can double-click the **Document Link** icon and see the page to which you are referring. This saves you from cutting and pasting information into your mail message. You can only create links in the rich text field (the body) of your mail message.

Links work the same way that hypertext works in the Help database (as you learned in Lesson 5) except that an icon represents the link. There are three types of Lotus Notes links that you can create and include in your mail messages or Lotus Notes documents, as shown in Table 15.1.

Table 15.1　Types of Links

This Icon	Named	Does This
	Document Link	Connects to another Lotus Notes document. It can be a mail message or a document within an entirely different database. Double-clicking a document link causes the linked document to appear on the screen.
	Database Link	Connects to another database opened at its default view.
	View Link	Connects to another database view (other than the default view).
	Anchor Link	Connects to a specific location in another document.

It's important to understand that links work only when they are linked to documents, views, and databases to which other users have access. If you link to a document that has been deleted or to a database not available to or accessible by the person to whom you are sending the link, it simply won't work.

Document Links

The examples in this lesson create links to the Help database. Be sure to use the server copy of the Help database, not a local copy. If you have access to discussion databases or other types of Lotus Notes databases, try these exercises, using those databases instead of the Help database.

To create a document link, do the following:

1. Begin a mail message by filling in the header (address, subject line, and so on) information.

2. In the body field of your message, type a sentence telling the recipient what information is in the document that's linked to your mail memo (this is a courtesy, not a requirement). You might type something such as **I'm learning how to create a document link. If you want to learn how to, click here.**

3. Press the **Spacebar** at the end of your sentence. Choose **Window**, **Workspace** from the menu to return to your workspace area without exiting this mail message.

4. Double-click the **Help** database icon to open the database. Do a quick search for Doclinks. Double-click to open the Creating a Link document.

5. With the Help document open, choose **Edit**, **Copy as Link**, **Document Link** from the menu.

6. To paste your newly created document link into your mail message choose **Window**, **New Memo** from the menu to return to your memo.

7. Place your cursor at the end of your sentence, remembering to leave the blank space. Choose **Edit**, **Paste** to insert the Document Link icon into your mail message (see Figure 15.1).

8. Send your mail message. Press **Esc** to close the Help database.

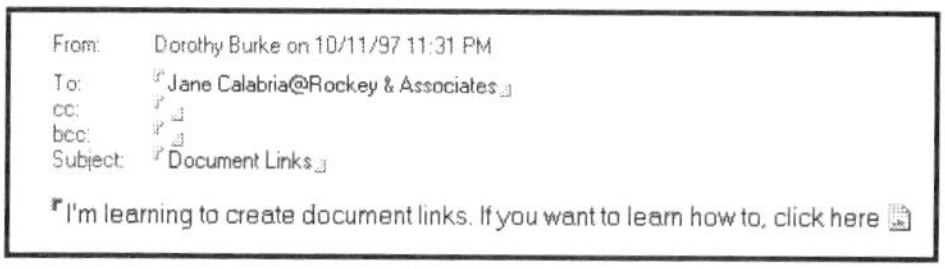

FIGURE 15.1 A document link within a mail message.

You can see the results of your document link by opening the Sent view of your mailbox and double-clicking the copy of the mail message you just created. If you want to display the name of the linked document, point at the Document Link icon and hold your mouse pointer there without clicking. A small hand appears, pointing at the Link icon. The name of the linked document appears, as shown in Figure 15.2.

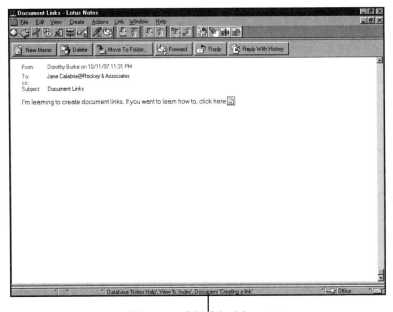

The name of the linked document

FIGURE 15.2   Point your mouse pointer at the Link icon to display the name of the linked document.

If you want to see the linked document, click the **Document Link** icon.

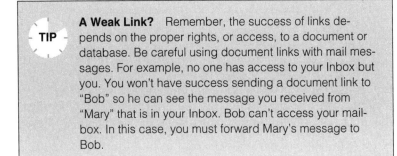

A Weak Link?   Remember, the success of links depends on the proper rights, or access, to a document or database. Be careful using document links with mail messages. For example, no one has access to your Inbox but you. You won't have success sending a document link to "Bob" so he can see the message you received from "Mary" that is in your Inbox. Bob can't access your mailbox. In this case, you must forward Mary's message to Bob.

Lotus Notes automatically creates document links when you use the reply option of Mail. Look in your Inbox and locate a mail message you've received as a reply. It's easy to identify replies— the subject line always starts with Re:. Double-click to open a reply. You see a document link located at the end of the subject line. Lotus Notes automatically places that document link; it points to the message to which this message is replying. Click (DL), the document link, and you can see the original message. This is an extremely helpful Mail tool that enables you to easily work your way back through the path of mail messages.

One quick way to see the linked document without clicking on the Document Link icon is to choose **View**, **Document Link Preview** from the menu. The linked document appears in a Preview pane at the bottom of the screen.

Anchor Links

When you create links to longer documents, it might help to have the link open the document to a particular location; this helps the recipient determine exactly what you want them to see without scanning several pages of superfluous information. You can accomplish this by creating an anchor link. To create an anchor link, do the following:

1. Begin a mail message by filling in the header (address, subject line, and so on) information.

2. In the body field of your message, type a sentence telling the recipient what information is available when he clicks the anchor link.

3. Press the **Spacebar** at the end of your sentence. Choose **Window**, **Workspace** from the menu to return to your workspace area without exiting this mail message.

4. Double-click the database icon where the document is stored to open that database. Select the appropriate view and then double-click the document to open it.

5. Change to edit mode by pressing **Ctrl+E**, by double-clicking the document, or by clicking the **Actions Edit**

Document SmartIcon. Move your insertion point (cursor) to the location in the document to which you want to link.

6. Choose **Edit**, **Copy as Link**, **Anchor Link** from the menu. A dialog box appears. Enter the anchor link text in the Anchor box and click **OK**. A small Anchor Link icon appears in the document. Save the document.

7. The next step is to paste the link into your mail message. Choose **Window**, **New Memo** from the menu to return to your memo.

8. Place your cursor at the end of your sentence, remembering to leave the blank space. Choose **Edit**, **Paste** to insert the Anchor Link icon into your mail message.

9. Send your mail message.

DATABASE LINKS

A database link connects to the default view of another database. To create a database link:

1. Begin a mail message by filling in the header (address, subject line, and so on) information.

2. In the body field of your message, type a sentence telling the recipient what information your document link contains.

3. Press the **Spacebar** at the end of your sentence. Choose **Window**, **Workspace** from the menu to return to your workspace area without exiting this mail message.

4. Click the database icon to select it (it's not necessary to open the database).

5. Choose **Edit**, **Copy as Link**, **Database Link** from the menu.

6. Choose **Window**, **New Memo** from the menu to return to your memo.

7. Place your cursor at the end of your sentence, remembering to leave the blank space. Choose **Edit, Paste** to insert the Database Link icon into your mail message.

8. Send your message.

You can test this link by looking at your copy of the sent message in Sent mail. When you double-click a database link, it opens the default view of the database.

VIEW LINKS

A view link works similarly to document links and database links, but opens a view instead of a document or database. To create a view link, follow the previous steps, but open the view to which you want to link when you copy your view link. Choose **Edit, Copy as Link, View Link** as your menu commands.

CREATING POP-UPS

A *Text Pop-Up hotspot* displays pop-up text. This is handy when you send information to several people, and only parts of that information are needed by some of those people. For example, if you're including terms that all the recipients won't understand, you can put the definitions in text pop-ups. Those recipients who need the definitions can click a word and additional text appears with the explanation of the term, as seen in Figure 15.3.

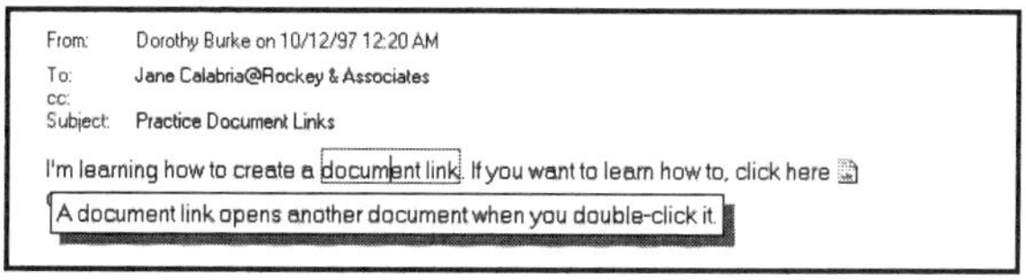

FIGURE 15.3   A text pop-up hotspot.

A text pop-up can be created only in the rich text field (body) of your mail message. To create this kind of hotspot, do the following:

1. Begin a mail message by filling in the header information.

2. In the body of the mail message, type your message. Determine which word(s) you want to become the text hotspot word (Figure 15.3 uses **document link**).

3. Highlight that word by selecting it with your mouse. Choose **Create**, **Hotspot**, **Text Pop-Up** from the menu.

4. The Text Pop-up Properties box appears, as shown in Figure 15.4.

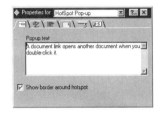

FIGURE 15.4   The HotSpot Pop-Up Properties box.

5. In the **Popup Text** box, fill in the text you want to pop up when this hotspot is clicked. Click the green check mark.

6. Close the Properties box. Finish and send your message.

You can see the effects of your pop-up by looking at the copy of your message in Sent mail.

LINK HOTSPOTS

Instead of placing an icon in your document, you can highlight text and make that a hotspot so that it appears much like Hypertext links on the Web. When you're creating your mail memo, you switch to the database, view, or document to which you want to link and create the link by using the **Edit**, **Copy as Link** commands. When you return to your mail memo, select the text you want to make the hotspot and choose **Create**, **Hotspot**,

Hotspot Link from the menu. The recipient can point and click that hotspot to open the database, view, or document to which you linked.

In this lesson, you learned how to create document links and how to follow the path of a mail reply by using document links. You also learned how to create text pop-ups. In the next lesson, you will learn how to create stationery and choose letterhead.

16

USING MAIL TOOLS

In this lesson, you learn how to create stationery, select letterhead, and activate an Out of Office Message. You also learn how to send a phone message and a serial route message.

CREATING STATIONERY

You can use stationery time and time again. You design how you want your stationary to look, including graphics and even a list of recipients. Stationery is stored in your Drafts folder, and you can create as many different stationery designs as you need. Most stationery is based on the Personal Stationery template, as are the instructions in this chapter. Different from the Mail Memo template, the Personal Stationery template has a total of three rich text fields to support graphics and formatting at the top and the bottom of the document.

To create stationery:

1. Open your mail database and choose **Actions**, **Mail Tools**, **Create Stationery** from the menu.

2. In the Create Stationery dialog box (see Figure 16.1), select the **Personal Stationery** template. Click **OK**.

3. Fill in the first rich text field, adding graphics or format-ted text. This field acts as a sort of "letterhead" field.

4. Fill in the To field and any other fields and text you want to appear each time you use this form. The last field is a rich text field in which you can include graphics and text formatting.

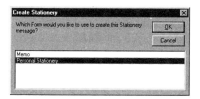

FIGURE 16.1   The Create Stationery dialog box.

5. To deliver this message with options other than the defaults, click the **Delivery Options** button on the Action bar to set your preferences.

6. Click the **Close** button on the Action bar. You're asked if you want to save this as stationery; choose **Yes**.

7. The Save As Stationery dialog box appears, as shown in Figure 16.2. Enter a name for the stationery in the What Would You Like to Call This Stationery? box.

FIGURE 16.2   Enter a name for the template.

8. The Save as Stationery dialog box appears (see Figure 16.3), confirming that the Stationery has been saved in your Drafts folder. Click **OK** to save and close the form.

FIGURE 16.3   The Save as Stationery dialog box.

The body field of the Personal Stationery template is the same field type as the Mail Message template. This is a rich text field. Figure 16.4 is an example of a Personal Stationery template with a formatted heading, a horizontal rule, and a table in the body field for recipients to supply sales-call information. With this kind of "design" leverage, you can use your stationery for many reports, such as weekly expense or sales reports.

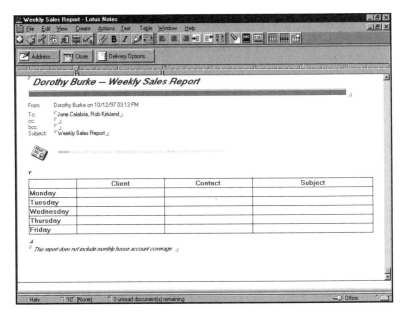

FIGURE 16.4   Personal Stationery created with a table in the rich text field.

To use your new stationery, go to the Drafts view, select the stationery, and click the **Use Stationery** button on the Action bar. A new mail message appears, including the elements you incorporated into your template. Enter your message and send it as you would any other mail message.

To change your stationery design, select it from the Drafts view and click the **Edit Document** button on the Action bar. Make your changes and save the document. To delete stationery, select it in your Drafts view and press the **Delete** key.

CHOOSING LETTERHEAD

If you don't like the way your name appears at the top of your mail memos, you can select from a variety of available styles. After you select a new look, called letterhead, you can change it at any time. To select letterhead, complete the following steps:

1. Open your mail database. Choose **Actions**, **Mail Tools**, **Choose Letterhead**.

2. The Choose Letterhead window appears, as shown in Figure 16.5. Scroll through the list to see which letterhead you want to use. The letterhead appears on your screen as you scroll through the list.

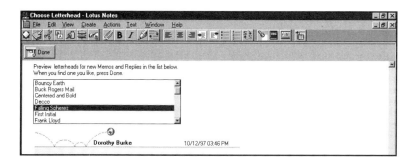

FIGURE 16.5 The Choose Letterhead window.

3. When you find the letterhead you like, click the **Done** button on the Action bar.

4. Create a new mail message to view your new letterhead.

To change your letterhead, follow steps 1–4 for selecting letterhead.

To go back to the original Mail Message form with no letterhead, follow steps 1–4, and select **Plain Text** as the type of letterhead.

Using the Out of Office Message

The Out of Office message enables you to respond to incoming mail messages while you are away from the office. Create a standard message that will be automatically sent as a response to incoming messages, notifying others that you are away. This is a good tool to use when you are away from the office for long periods of time without access to your mail. You can even create a unique response message to individuals or groups so that some people receive one type of response, and others receive a different response.

To create an Out of Office message, do the following:

1. Open your mail database. Choose **Actions**, **Mail Tools**, **Out of Office** from the menu.

2. The Out of Office Profile form appears. There are four sections to this form. In the first section, add the dates for **Leaving** and **Returning**. Figure 16.6 shows those fields.

3. The second section provides a place for you to type your Out of Office message that will be delivered to "most" people. This will actually be delivered to all people, unless you indicate otherwise in sections 3 and 4. Type your message in this section, as shown in Figure 16.7.

4. (**Optional**) Section 3 enables you to provide a message for a special person or a group of people. To select people for this group, press the down arrow key. When the dialog box appears, select people from your address book, as shown in Figure 16.7.

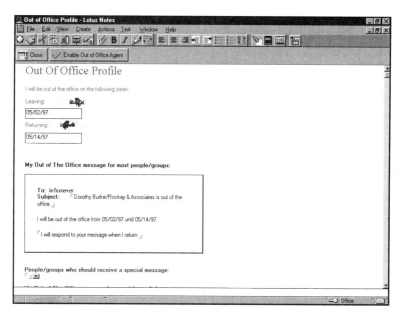

FIGURE 16.6   Out of Office Profile form with Leaving and Returning dates.

5. Type your special message in the My Out of the Office Message for Special People/Groups section, as shown in Figure 16.8.

6. The fourth section enables you to list people who should not receive any notification at all. Click the drop-down arrow key and select people or groups for this field, or leave it blank.

7. Click the **Enable Out of Office Agent** button on the Action bar. A dialog box confirms that the agent is enabled. Click the **OK** button.

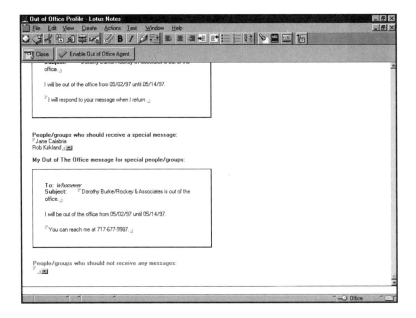

FIGURE 16.7 The special message and the people selected to receive it.

If you return to the office on the date that you indicated in the Out of Office Profile form, you don't need to disable Out of Office. If you return before that date, disable the message with the following steps:

1. Open your mail database. Choose **Actions**, **Mail Tools**, **Out of Office** from the menu.

2. When the Out of Office Profile form appears, click the **I Have Returned to the Office** button located on the Action bar.

Don't Forget to Replicate! If you are a remote user and you have created an Out Of Office message from your remote PC, be certain to replicate your Mail database before leaving for your trip. Otherwise, the server will not be notified that this agent needs to run. Refer to Lesson 23 for remote user information.

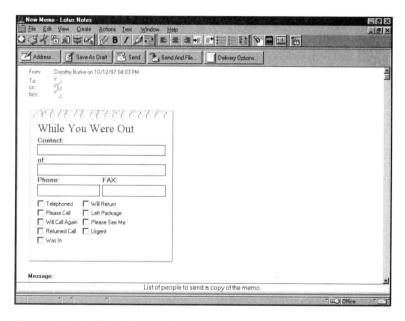

FIGURE 16.8   The Phone Message form.

CREATING PHONE MESSAGES

Phone messages are simple, straightforward forms used to send telephone message information via Notes. Phone messages work in the same manner as mail messages—fill out the form, click the Send button on the Action bar, and the message is mailed to the person or person in the To cc and bcc fields. To create a phone message.

1. Open your mail database, or click the mail database icon once to select it.

2. Choose **Create**, **Special**, **Phone Message** from the menu.

3. The Phone Message form appears, as shown in Figure 16.8. Fill in the To field and any other information you want to supply with this message.

4. Use the rich text field, **Message**, to type any additional information that the caller supplied with his message.

5. Click the **Send** button on the Action bar to send the message.

CREATING SERIAL ROUTE MESSAGES

Mail provides the capability to route messages. Different than a distribution list or a list of names in the To, cc, bcc fields, a routed message is delivered to recipients in the order that you indicate. For example, if you are mailing expense reports through Lotus Notes Mail, serial routing gives you the ability to submit the report first to your manager, then to her manager, and then to the accounting department.

A Serial Route message is routed to each person listed in the Route To field of the memo in the order in which you place people's names. You can address this memo to a list of individuals only; you can't use groups that you created in your address book. To create a Serial Route message, do the following:

1. Open your mail database, or select it in your workspace by clicking the mail database icon.

2. Choose **Create**, **Special**, **Serial Route Memo** from the menu.

3. The Serial Route Memo does not have a cc or bcc field. Fill in the Route To field with the names of those you want to route in the order that you want to route to them.

4. If you want to be notified of the delivery of this message to each recipient as he receives it, click the **Notify Sender at Each Stop** box.

5. Click the **Send** button in the Action bar to send this message.

When you receive a Serial Route Memo, open and read it, and then click the **Send to Next Person** button on the Action bar to route it to the next person in the list.

In this lesson, you learned how to create and customize stationery and select letterhead. You also learned how to create, enable, and disable an Out of Office message. In the next lesson, you will learn how to use Lotus Notes workflow options.

LESSON 17

USING TASKS

In this lesson, you learn how to use tasks, keep track of your personal To Do list, and assign tasks to others.

CREATING TASKS

To help keep track of all the things you have to do, you can assign tasks to yourself. For example, if you know you have a presentation to give in two weeks, you can assign a task to yourself, noting all the things you must prepare by that date. To create a task, do the following:

1. Open your mail database. Choose **Create**, **Task** from the menu, or if you're in the To Do view, click the **New Task** button on the Action bar. The New Task form appears, as shown in Figure 17.1.

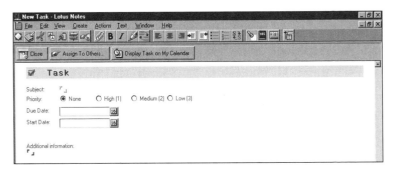

FIGURE 17.1 The New Task form.

2. Enter a description of the task under Subject.

3. To set a priority for the task, click **High**, **Medium**, or **Low** (the default is **None**).

4. Enter a date in the Due Date box to set a due date for the task or click the **Date** icon next to the box to select a date from the drop-down calendar.

5. To establish a start date for the task, enter the date in the Start Date box or click the **Date** icon next to the box to select a date from the drop-down calendar.

6. (**Optional**) In Additional Information, add any information needed to explain the task or how it is to be completed.

7. (**Optional**) If you want to add the Task to your Calendar so that the due date appears as an entry, click the Display Task on My Calendar button on the Action bar.

8. Click the **Close** button on the Action bar.

9. When the alert box appears, asking if you want to save the document, choose **Yes**.

10. The task appears in your To Do view. Click the **To Do** button in the Navigator pane to see a list of tasks.

You also can assign tasks to others. For example, if you and your staff are planning to attend a convention, you can assign tasks to each member of your staff. To assign tasks to others, do the following:

1. Follow steps 1–5 of assigning a task to yourself.

2. Click the **Assign to Others** button on the Action bar. Two new fields appear on the form (see Figure 17.2).

3. In the Assign To field, enter the name of the person to whom you are assigning the task. Click the **Address** button on the Action bar if you want to look up the name in one of the address books.

4. Put the names of anyone who should receive a copy of this task in the cc field.

5. In Additional Information, add any information to explain the task or how it is to be completed.

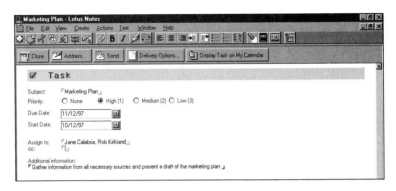

FIGURE 17.2   A task being assigned to others.

6. Click the **Send** button on the Action bar (click **Close** instead, if you want to save the task without sending it). Because this sends a mail message to the person assigned to the task, you can assign any of the Delivery Options before sending the message.

CONVERTING TASKS

Convert mail messages to Tasks so that they appear in your To Do list. For example, converting a mail message from your manager that asks you to prepare your department's budget for next year to a task adds that message to your To Do list so that you won't forget to follow up. To convert a mail message to a task, do the following:

1. Select the document in the View pane or open the message.

2. Choose **Actions**, **Convert to Task**.

3. The mail message appears as a Task document, and you can make any changes or additions you want to the information provided there.

4. If you want to assign the task to yourself, click the **Close** button on the Action bar, or press the **Esc** key.

To assign the task to anyone else, click the **Assign to Others** button on the Action bar, fill in the Assign To and cc fields, and then click the **Send** button on the Action bar.

You also can create new tasks from Calendar entries. If you're creating an entry that also happens to be the deadline for a task, choose **Actions**, **Copy Into**, **New Task** from the menu. Change any information in the New Task document and then save and close it.

Existing tasks often generate new tasks, and you can create new tasks from an existing task document. With the existing task selected or open, choose **Actions**, **Copy Into**, **New Task** from the menu. Complete the new task document, save it, and close it.

VIEWING TASK STATUS

To keep track of the tasks you assign to yourself, tasks others assign to you, and tasks you assign to others, open the To Do view in the Mail database.

The To Do view divides the tasks into Completed, Current, Future, Overdue, and Today categories. It also displays messages that ask you to respond by a particular date.

MARKING A COMPLETED TASK

When a task is completed, mark it so. Marking a task as completed moves the task into the Complete category of the To Do view. If someone else assigned the task to you, that person gets a message showing that you completed the task.

To mark a task as complete, do the following:

1. From the To Do view, select or open the task.

2. Click the **Mark Completed** button on the Action bar. The task moves under the Completed area in the To Do view (see Figure 17.3).

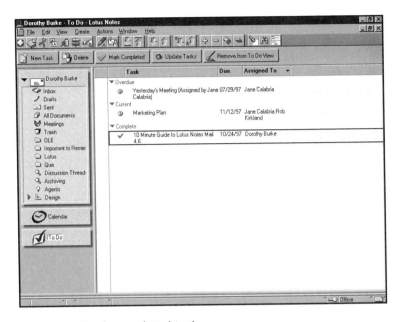

FIGURE 17.3   A completed task.

When you open a task to mark it complete, you receive a prompt, asking if you want to send additional comments to the person who assigned the task to you. If you select **No**, the task is marked as completed and a message is sent to the person who assigned the task to you. If you select **Yes**, a mail memo appears, addressed to the person who assigned the task. Complete the mail memo and click the **Send** button.

UPDATING STATUS

After a task is created, Notes does not read the task and check the dates constantly. For a task to move from the Current category to the Overdue category, you must update the status manually or automatically.

The manual method is as follows:

1. Open your mail database in the To Do view.

2. Click the **Update Tasks** button on the Action bar.

Notes reads the dates of the tasks and recategorizes them if necessary.

The automatic method is as follows:

1. Open the Agents view of your mail database (see Figure 17.4).

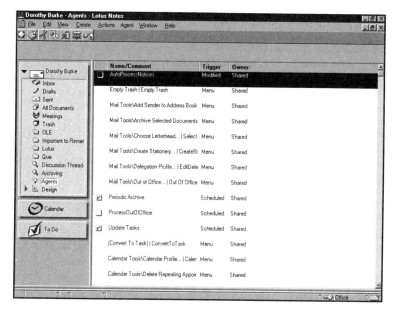

FIGURE 17.4   The Agents view.

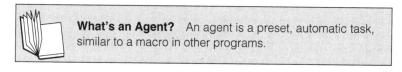

What's an Agent?   An agent is a preset, automatic task, similar to a macro in other programs.

2. Check the box in front of **Update Tasks**.

Which Server? You might be asked on which server you want the agent to run. If your mail is stored on the Notes server, choose your mail server; you might not have access to run an agent on that server, so check with your Notes administrator before doing this. If you're a remote user and your mail is stored on your own PC, select **Local**. Some additional settings might be required if you choose Local, and you should consult your Notes administrator on running this agent locally.

3. Lotus Notes schedules the Update Tasks agent to run each night at 1:00 A.M., unless you change the time.

In this lesson, you learned how to assign tasks to yourself and to others, how to mark the tasks as completed, how to view the tasks, and how to update the task list. In the next lesson, you will learn how to use your Calendar.

SETTING UP TO USE THE CALENDAR

In this lesson, you learn how to view and use your Calendar entries. You also learn how to enable others to see your free time and calendar, as well as how to permit others to read your mail.

CONFIGURING OPTIONS

Calendaring and scheduling enables you to keep track of your time, check availability of other Notes users, and easily see a list of meeting invitations sent to you. With the calendar features, you can do the following:

- Make appointments on your personal calendar

- View your calendar in two-days, one-week, two-weeks, or one-month views

- Schedule meetings and invite others

- View the free time of other Notes users

- Enter repeating or multi-day appointments (such as monthly meetings or vacations)

- Create a reminder to yourself that appears in your calendar

- Enter anniversary information (appointments which repeat weekly, month, yearly, and so on)

- Schedule rooms and resources for your meetings

Free Time   Enables you to view available time (time not blocked out by appointments) of other Notes users. This is not the same as viewing the calendar itself. For example, if you want to invite John Baker to a meeting, you can look up his free time to see when he is available. If John keeps his calendar current in Notes, viewing his schedule helps you ensure that John isn't otherwise "booked" during your proposed meeting time. For more information on viewing Free Time, see Lesson 19, "Using the Calendar."

Your calendar and the information it contains are stored and viewed in your mail database. Two views are available for scheduling information:

- **Calendar view**   Displays appointments you make and meeting information for meetings you have accepted, in a two-day, one-week, two-week, or one-month format (see Figure 18.1).

- **Meetings view**   Lists meeting invitations and meetings you have accepted by date and meeting time (see Figure 18.2).

Two documents in your mail database enable you to administer your calendaring and scheduling functions and to determine what calendar and mail information you want to share with others. They are the Calendar Profile and the Delegation Profile. Table 18.1 describes the sharing options you can select.

Click to scroll up and down times   Click to go to a specified date

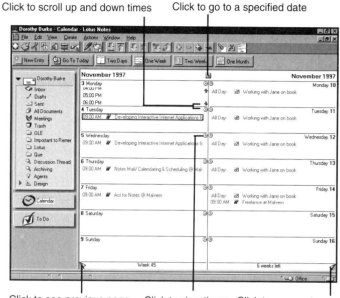

Click to see previous page   Click to view times   Click to see next page

FIGURE 18.1   The Calendar view in the Two Week format.

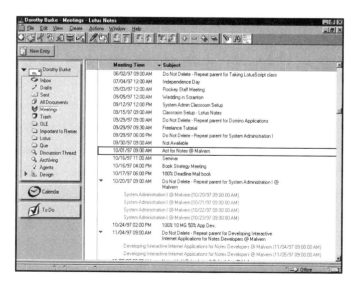

FIGURE 18.2   The Meetings view.

TABLE 18.1   HOW YOU CAN SHARE CALENDAR AND MAIL
INFORMATION

IN THE CALENDAR PROFILE	IN THE DELEGATION PROFILE, ENTER WHO CAN:
See your free time	Read your calendar
	Manage your calendar
	Read your mail
	Read and send mail on your behalf
	Read, send, and edit any document in your mail database
	Delete mail in your mail database
	Automatically schedule you for meetings

SETTING YOUR CALENDAR PROFILE

The Calendar Profile document must be completed before you
can work with your calendar. Your Notes administrator might
have completed this step for you. If you click your Calendar view
and receive a message that your Profile must be set, complete the
steps that follow. Or, simply follow the steps to confirm the information contained in your Calendar Profile document (see Figure
18.3).

Check with your Notes administrator to confirm that the information you enter in the Calendar Profile and the Delegation Profile agrees with your Notes setup at work. To configure the
Calendar Profile:

1. From the workspace, select or open your mail database.

2. Choose **Actions, Calendar Tools, Calendar Profile**
   from the menu.

3. Confirm that your name appears in the Mail File Owner
   field.

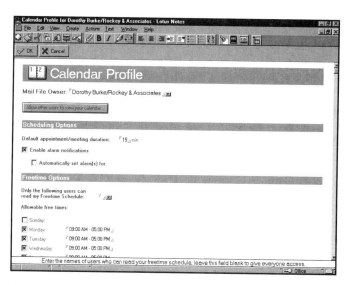

FIGURE 18.3   The Calendar Profile document.

4. If you want to allow others see your calendar, click **Allow Other Users to View Your Calendar** and open the Delegation Profile document. (This document is explained in the next section. If you want to allow others to view your calendar, stop here, go to the instructions for the Delegation Profile, and go to step 5, which follows.) If you do not want others to access your calendar, go to step 5 now.

TIP   **Let Others See My Calendar?**   No way! Allowing others to see your calendar is very different from allowing others to see your free time. Be careful with this selection. If you allow others to see your calendar, they will see appointments you've entered into your calendar, except for those you specifically mark as **Not for public viewing**. Also note that viewing your calendar is not the same as viewing your mail, even though the Calendar view is found in the mail database. You also can give people access to your mail. See "Setting Your Delegation Profile" in this lesson.

5. In the Scheduling Options portion of this document, enter your Default Appointment/Meeting Duration. This is the number of minutes you want as the interval between times on your calendar. The default setting is 60 minutes.

6. Check the **Enable Alarm Notifications** option if you want to be alerted to upcoming events, appointments, meetings, and so on.

7. Check the **Automatically Set Alarm(s) For** option and then check **Appointments/Meetings**, **Reminders**, **Events**, or **Anniversaries** to select which you want to receive notification of. Also enter the amount of advance notice you want.

8. To restrict who can view your free time (see Figure 18.4), click the down arrow next to the **Only the Following Users Can Read My Freetime Shedule** field and add only the names of people whom you want to see your free time. Leaving this field blank allows *all* Notes users on your server to see your free time. (The purpose of group scheduling is to allow others to see your free time. It is suggested that you leave this field blank.)

TIP **Revealing Your Free Time** You can select from the Personal or Public Address Books when entering names of those whom you want to see your free time.

---

9. Enter your Allowable Free Times. Check the days you are available for scheduling, and enter your available hours for each of the days you selected (the default setting is 09:00 A.M. to 05:00 P.M.).

Under the Advanced Calendar Options section (see Figure 18.5), you see a subsection called Autoprocessing Options.

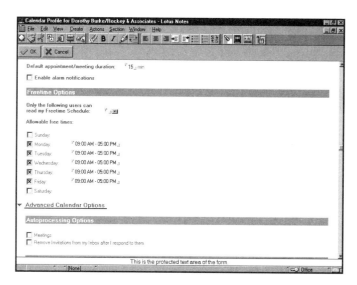

FIGURE 18.4   Scroll down the Calendar Profile to see the Freetime Options.

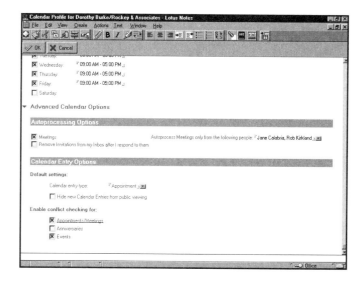

FIGURE 18.5   The Advanced Calendar Options section.

Selecting Autoprocessing options instructs Notes to automatically add information to your calendar. Select the following options, as you desire:

- **Meetings** Meeting invitations are automatically accepted and added to your calendar when you select this option but only if the invitation is sent by those you specified in the field called Autoprocess Meetings Only from the Following People. Enter names into this field by typing the names or selecting them from the Names dialog box, which is a list of people in the Personal or Public Address Book.

- **Remove Invitations from My Inbox after I Respond to Them** Check this box to delete meeting invitations from the Inbox view after you have accepted or rejected the invitation.

- **Default Settings** Select the Calendar entry type you want to automatically appear when you are making entries.

- **Hide New Calendar Entries from Public Viewing** Check to prevent everyone else from seeing your new entries.

- **Enable Conflict Checking For** Select the items you don't want to be in conflict so that Notes alerts you if they overlap.

When you have completed the information, save the Calendar Profile document by clicking **OK** on the Action bar or by clicking **Cancel** to exit the document without saving it.

SETTING YOUR DELEGATION PROFILE

The Delegation Profile enables you to specify who may view your calendar and who may make entries for you. You can also use this document to designate who may read your mail or send mail on your behalf.

To create a Delegation Profile document (see Figure 18.6), choose **Actions**, **Mail Tools**, **Delegation Profile** from the menu or click the **Allow Other Users to View Your Calendar** button in the Calendar Profile document.

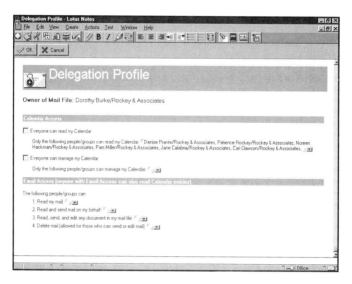

FIGURE 18.6   The Delegation Profile document.

Complete the appropriate fields in the Delegation Profile:

- **Everyone Can Read My Calendar**   Check this only if you mean it! Checking this field allows access to your calendar by every Notes user on your server. Leave this field without a check mark and if you want, enter the names of those people who can view your calendar in Only the Following People/Groups Can Read My Calendar.

- **Everyone Can Manage My Calendar**   Check this only if you mean it! Checking this field gives the rights to change your calendar to every Notes user on your server. To restrict who can manage your calendar, leave this field without a check mark and enter the names of the people who can modify your calendar entries in Only the Following People/Groups Can Manage My Calendar.

In the E-mail Access section of the form, you can specify who can read your mail; read and send mail on your behalf; read, send, and edit documents in your mail database; or delete your mail. Enter or select names in the appropriate fields to grant this permission.

When you are ready, save the Delegation Profile document by clicking **OK** on the Action bar or by clicking **Cancel** to exit the document without saving it.

TIP **Reading Someone Else's Calendar**   When you have access to read another person's calendar, you open it by choosing **Actions**, **Calendar Tools**, **Open Another Calendar**. In the Open Calendar dialog box, select the address book in which the other user is listed and then click the user's name. Click **OK**. Press the **Esc** key when you're finished viewing the calendar.

In this lesson, you learned how to configure your Calendar and Delegation preferences for your mail and your calendar. In the next lesson, you will learn how to create appointments, view Free Time, and respond to invitations.

USING THE
CALENDAR

19

*In this lesson, you learn how to
make entries in your calendar. You
also learn how to accept meeting
invitations and how to check the available time of others.*

MAKING CALENDAR ENTRIES

As explained in Lesson 18, "Setting Up to Use the Calendar," entries that you make in your calendar affect your free time availability. Although others might not be able to view your *calendar*, they might be able to view your *free time*. Check with your Notes administrator if you have difficulty seeing the free time of others. There are several types of calendar entries you can create:

- **Appointment** is a meeting with a client or a personal appointment such as a doctor's visit. You cannot invite others to an appointment. An appointment has a time value (2:00 to 3:00), and it can repeat or occur only once.

- **Invitation** is an appointment in which you want to include and invite others. Those you invite must be part of your Notes Mail system and Notes automatically notifies them for you by sending them an invitation in their mail. It is possible that you might also find cc:Mail users and Office Vision users in your Invitation list if your systems administrator configured Lotus Notes to include them.

- **Event** has a duration that lasts for more than one day, such as a vacation. Events can occur for a number of consecutive days, or they can be repeated (see **Repeat**, later in this lesson, for more information).

- **Reminder** is a note to yourself that displays on your calendar at the time and date you assign to it.

- **Anniversary** is a repeating occasion that you want to appear on your calendar weekly, monthly, or yearly.

You can create a calendar entry at any time while in Lotus Notes, and you don't have to have the mail database open. To create a calendar entry, do one of the following:

> **From anywhere in Notes**   Choose **Create**, **Mail**, **Calendar Entry** from the menu.

> **From within the Mail database**   Choose **Create**, **Calendar Entry** from the menu.

> **From your Calendar view in Mail**   Click the **New Entry** button on the Action bar or double-click a date or time slot in the calendar.

Follow these instructions to complete the calendar entry:

1. Select the type of entry you want to create: Appointment, Invitation, Event, Reminder, or Anniversary. Depending upon the type of calendar entry you choose, the entry fields vary slightly (see Figures 19.1 and 19.2).

Figure 19.1   An Appointment entry.

FIGURE 19.2 An Event entry.

2. Enter information in the fields in the document. The remaining fields on the document vary slightly, depending on the type of entry you have selected:

> **Brief Description**   Enter the text that is to appear in the Calendar view as the title of the Calendar entry.

> **Date**   Enter the date or click the **Calendar** button to see a miniature calendar. Use the left and right arrows at the top of the calendar to move from month to month. Click on the day to select the date. Figure 19.3 shows the miniature calendar.

FIGURE 19.3 Choosing a date.

> **Time** (does not appear for Anniversary or Event)   Enter the time or click the **Clock** button to see a time scale (see Figure 19.4). Drag the indicators up or down the scale to set the time and duration of the appointment. Use the up and down triangles to see different parts of the scale. Click the green check mark to accept the time setting.

FIGURE 19.4   Setting a time.

Duration (appears only for Event)   Enter the number of days the event will last.

Detailed Description   Enter a brief description of the appointment.

Reservations (appears only for Invitation)   Three options appear in the Reservations section: You can reserve any available room, a specific room, or resources such as a projector or computer. These options might not be enabled in your company. Speak to your Notes administrator regarding this section of the form.

Pencil In   This option marks the entry on your calendar, but does not affect your free time.

Not for Public Viewing   Prevents others from seeing this appointment if you have chosen to allow others to view your calendar in your calendar profile. Use this if you want to enter a confidential or personal appointment, such as a doctor's visit. Others can see that your line is blocked out but cannot see the actual appointment.

3. Use the **Repeat** button on the Action bar for appointments that occur on more than one date, such as a
monthly meeting. In the Repeat Rules dialog box (see
Figure 19.5), select the **Repeat** interval from the drop-
down list. Based on that choice, set the specifics of the
frequency and intervals. Then, set the **Starting Date**.
Choose **Until** and set the ending date or **For**, and then
set the length of time. Click **OK**.

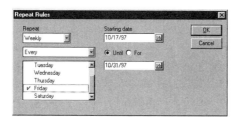

FIGURE 19.5   The Repeat Rules dialog box.

4. Click the **Alarm Options** button on the Action bar to
receive a reminder of this entry. In the Set Alarm dialog
box (see Figure 19.6), specify the number of **Minutes**,
choose **Before**, **After**, or **On** (to specify a specific date
and time), and enter an **Alarm Message**. Click **OK**.

If you set a default appointment alarm in the Calendar
profile (see Lesson 18) and don't want an alarm for this
appointment, check **Turn Alarm Off** in the Alarm
dialog box and then click **OK**.

5. Click the **Save and Close** button on the Action bar to
save your entry.

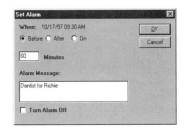

FIGURE 19.6   The Set Alarm dialog box.

VIEWING FREE TIME

When you invite others to a meeting, you can check their free time by clicking the **Find Free Time** button in the invitations section of your calendar entry. To create a calendar entry, invite others, and see their free time, follow these steps:

1. From the Calendar view of your mail database, click the **New Entry** button on the Action bar.

2. Select **Invitation** as your calendar entry type.

3. Complete the **Brief Description**, **Date**, and **Time** fields. If appropriate, complete the **Detailed Description** field.

4. Complete the **Send Invitations To** field. If you would like to invite others whose attendance you do not require, enter their names into the **Optional Invitees** field. You can type the names in the field or click the down-arrow button to select the invitees from the Names dialog box.

5. Click the **Find Free Time** button to see the free time of the invitees. The Free Time dialog box appears, as shown in Figure 19.7. This box displays a white bar behind the name of each person whose free time is available for viewing (gray if it is not). Blue bars indicate busy times for

each person, and a red or green bar represents the appointment you are creating. If your appointment bar is green, the time is OK for everyone, and that information is displayed on the left of the Free Time dialog box. If there is a conflict in schedules, the dialog box displays **Scheduled time is not OK for everyone**, and the appointment bar is red.

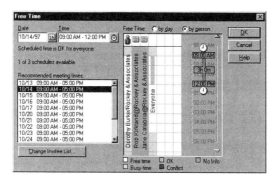

FIGURE 19.7   The Free Time dialog box.

6. If your scheduled time is not OK, you can change the **Date** and **Time** fields in the Free Time dialog box. You also can change the list of invitees by clicking the **Change Invitee List** button of the dialog box.

7. When you are satisfied with your meeting time and invitees, click **OK** to close the dialog box.

8. Click the **Save** and **Close** button on the Action bar to save this calendar entry. Notes sends invitations to those listed in your Required and Optional Invitee lists.

This meeting will now appear in your calendar.

RESPONDING TO INVITATIONS

Invitations that you receive from others appear in the Inbox view of your mail, as well as the Meetings view. Meetings only appear in your calendar if you created them yourself, gave someone else the rights to create them, or accepted an invitation. Figure 19.8 shows an invitation in the Inbox view of Mail.

	Jane Calabria	10/11/97	Please add a header to you TOC
	Jane Calabria	10/11/97	Page count
★	Jane Calabria	10/13/97	Invitation - Please come to the company Halloween brunch [31 Oct 12:15 AM EST]

FIGURE 19.8   An invitation in the Inbox.

To respond to an invitation, follow these steps:

1. Open the invitation by double-clicking it in your Meetings or Inbox view of Mail.

2. Select your response by using the buttons on the Action bar (see Figure 19.9). Those choices are as follows:

    Accept mails an acceptance notice to the person who initiated the invitation, adds the meeting to your Calendar and to your Meetings view, and marks that time as busy on your free time schedule.

    Decline sends a regrets notification to the person who initiated the invitation.

    Other gives you the option to **Accept** or **Decline** with comments, **Delegate** this meeting to someone else who you specify (who will be automatically notified), or **Propose Alternate Time/Location**. If you're not sure you can attend the meeting, select **Pencil In** in the **Action to Take** field.

3. Choose the appropriate selection and click **OK** to save and close the document.

Accept   Decline Other   Options dialog box

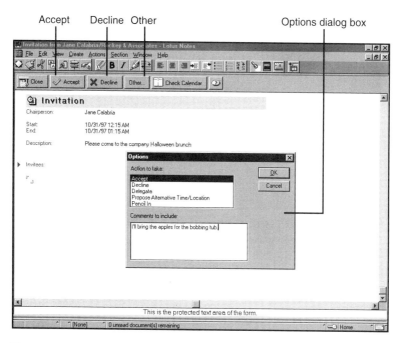

FIGURE 19.9   Responding to an invitation.

PRINTING THE CALENDAR

Having a calendar in Notes is really useful but not when you're away from your computer. In that case, you can print out your Calendar view, a list of Calendar entries, or one or more Calendar entries.

To print a Calendar view, do the following:

1. Switch to the Calendar view you want to print and display the dates you want on your printout.

2. Choose File, Print from the menu.

3. Under View Options in the File Print dialog box (see Figure 19.10), select Print View.

FIGURE 19.10   The File Print dialog box.

4. **(Optional)** To print more than one copy, specify the number in the **Copies** field.

5. Click **OK**.

To print a list of Calendar entries, follow steps 1 and 2. Then select **Print Selected Days** under the **View Options** in the File Print dialog box. Specify the first and last days you want to print in the **From** and **To** fields. Click **OK**.

Printing one or more Calendar entries is slightly different. You need to click the entry you want to print or hold down the **Shift** key and then click each entry to print more than one. When you're in the File Print dialog box, select **Print Selected Documents** from the **View Options**. Then click **OK**.

In this lesson, you learned how to create Calendar entries, invite others, and see the free time of others. You also learned how to respond to an invitation. In the next lesson, you will learn how to use the Favorites database.

UNDERSTANDING THE FAVORITES DATABASE

In this lesson, you learn what the Favorites database is and how it works. You also learn how to add databases to the Favorites navigator.

WHAT IS THE FAVORITES DATABASE?

In addition to your mail database, your Personal Address Book, and the Public Address Book, Lotus Notes adds three databases when you install it—a personal journal database, a Personal Web Navigator database, and the Favorites database, which is based upon the portfolio template.

A *portfolio* template enables a collection of database and view pointers to be contained within one database, acting as a map to your favorites. For example, instead of having to return to the workspace from your Mail database to open your Personal Address Book, the portfolio database contains buttons that you can use to navigate between the two databases.

The Favorites database (aptly named) contains buttons for your mail database, the Calendar view of your mail database, the To Do view of your mail database, your Personal Address Book, your Personal Journal database, and the Personal Web Navigator (which only appears if this is a fresh install of Notes or an upgrade in which you were using the Personal Web Navigator).

You can add additional databases or views to the portfolio at any time, as you learn later in this lesson.

MOVING AROUND THE FAVORITES WINDOW

To open the Favorites portfolio, double-click the Favorites icon on your workspace.

When you open the Favorites portfolio, Notes displays the documents from the mail database Inbox view in the View pane (see Figure 20.1). Buttons for the databases and mail views are in the Navigator pane. When you choose one of the views, you see the same documents as you do when you open the same database from its icon on the workspace.

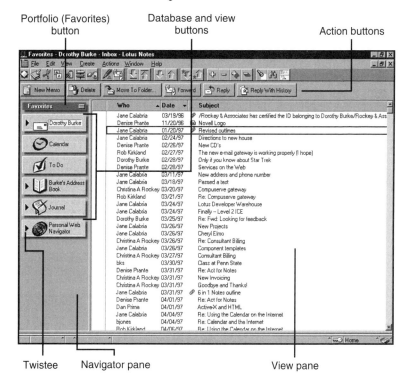

FIGURE 20.1   The Favorites window.

Some buttons are expandable, as indicated by small triangles. As with your mail database, you can use the Preview Pane button to show or hide the Preview pane.

Press the **Esc** key or choose **File**, **Close** to close the database and return to the workspace.

ADDING DATABASES TO FAVORITES

The Favorites portfolio is a one-stop shop for managing your frequently used databases. You can customize Favorites by adding other frequently used databases. To add a database to the Favorites portfolio, follow these steps:

1. Open the Favorites portfolio by double-clicking its icon on the workspace.

2. Click the **Favorites** name bar in the Navigator pane.

3. Choose **Edit Portfolio** from the pop-up menu. The Databases view appears (see Figure 20.2).

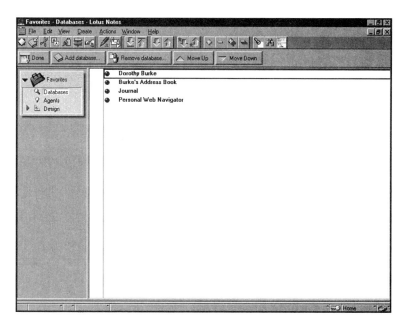

FIGURE 20.2   The Databases view.

4. Click the **Add Database** action button or choose **Actions**, **Add Database** from the menu. The Add Database to Portfolio dialog box opens (see Figure 20.3).

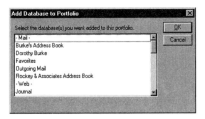

FIGURE 20.3   The Add Database to Portfolio dialog box.

5. The databases are listed by workspace page (you can't add a database to a portfolio unless it has a database icon displayed on a workspace page). Select one or more databases to add to Favorites by clicking once on the name of each database you want.

6. Click **OK**.

7. Click the **Done** action button to return to the previous view.

> **TIP** **Quickly Add Databases**   To quickly add databases to your Favorites portfolio, drag the icon of the database you want to add onto the Favorites icon.

If the database you want to add to your Favorites portfolio does not appear on a workspace page, follow these instructions to add that icon to a workspace page:

1. Return to the workspace by pressing the **Esc** key or choosing **File**, **Close** from the menu. Or, if you want to leave the Portfolio database open, switch to the workspace by choosing **Window**, **Workspace at Home** or **Window**, **Workspace at Office**.

2. Choose **File**, **Database**, **Open** from the menu. The Open Database dialog box appears (see Figure 20.4).

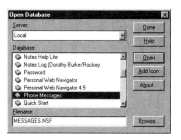

FIGURE 20.4   The Open Database dialog box.

3. From the Server drop-down list, select the computer where the database is stored. If it's stored on your own computer, choose **Local**. Otherwise, select the name of a server.

4. From the Database list, select the database you want (you can choose only one database at a time). If you're not sure which database to select because you don't recognize the name, click the **About** button to read the About Database document for the selected database. Click **Close** to return to the Open Database dialog box.

5. To add the icon to the current workspace page, click the **Add Icon** button. Then, click **Done**. If you want to open the database and add the icon, click **Open**.

The database icon appears on the current workspace page. Follow the instructions for adding it to your Favorites portfolio.

REMOVING A DATABASE FROM THE FAVORITES PORTFOLIO

When you decide that you no longer need a database in Favorites, you can remove it. This doesn't remove the icon from the workspace or delete the file from your disk, however. This process simply removes the button from the Favorites database.

To remove a database from Favorites, do the following:

1. Open the Favorites portfolio by double-clicking its icon on the workspace.

2. Click the **Favorites** name bar in the Navigator pane.

3. Choose **Edit Portfolio** from the pop-up menu. The Databases view opens.

4. In the View pane, select the name of the database you want to remove.

5. Click the **Remove Database** action button or choose **Actions**, **Remove Database** from the menu.

6. When a dialog box appears asking if you're sure, click **Yes**.

7. Click the **Done** action button to return to the previous view.

Rearranging Databases

Lotus Notes sets the order of the databases in the Navigator pane for you. To change that order, follow these instructions:

1. Open the Favorites portfolio by double-clicking its icon on the workspace.

2. Click the **Favorites** name bar in the Navigator pane.

3. Choose **Edit Portfolio** from the pop-up menu. The Databases view opens.

4. In the View pane, select the name of the database that you want to move up or down in the list.

5. Click the **Move Up** action button to move the database up the list or the **Move Down** action button to move the database down the list.

6. Click the **Done** action button when you have the arrangement you want.

When buttons are added to the Favorites database, you have the option of accessing databases from those buttons or opening them from the icons on your workspace.

In this lesson you learned how to view the information in the Favorites database and how to customize the database to suit your needs. In the next lesson you will learn about passwords, encrypting your mail, and the Access Control List.

21

UNDERSTANDING SECURITY

In this lesson, you learn about using and changing passwords, as well as Access Control Lists and how they affect you. You also learn how encryption and signatures protect your documents.

NOTES SECURITY

Lotus Notes and Domino security have several levels of access. Notes administrators and designers can determine the following:

- Who can access the server

- Who can access each database

- Who can access views and documents within a database

- Who can access fields within a form

Accessing the server is determined by your Notes ID and password. Whether or not you can access a database and what you can do within the database is determined by the Access Control List for each database. Notes security is a powerful, important tool for your company.

PASSWORDS

Your first line of defense in securing your system and mail from unauthorized people is your password. When you access the Domino server the first time, you start a Notes session, which prompts you to enter your password (see Figure 21.1). For security, neither you nor anyone else can see what you are typing—all you see are Xs.

FIGURE 21.1   Prompt for password.

Your password can be any combination of keyboard characters, as long as the first character is a letter of the alphabet. The number of characters in your password is determined when your Notes ID is created (by your Notes administrator). Note that because passwords are case sensitive, the password "INFONUT" is different from the password "infonut."

You can change your password at any time, by doing the following:

1. Choose **File**, **Tools**, **User ID** from the menu.

2. Enter your current password, if you are asked, and then click **OK**.

3. Click the **Set Password** button.

4. Enter your current password and click **OK**.

5. Enter the new password and click **OK**.

6. To confirm your password, type the new password again, exactly as you did the first time.

7. Click **OK**.

8. Click **Done**.

Someone Is Accessing My Mail!   Don't give your password to others. And never give your User ID file to others! If someone has your ID, changing your password will not stop him from accessing your mail because the password is stored in the User ID file. For further security, it's also a good idea to change the password assigned to you by your Notes administrator. Typically, the administrator assigns a password that is easy for him (and you) to remember; this initial password is left easy so that you can get up and running on Notes. It's not unusual for that password to be the same password assigned to all Notes users. Shortly after you become familiar with Notes, take the time to change your password and keep it to yourself!

The User ID is a file created when the Notes administrator first registers you as a user. When you start up Lotus Notes on your computer for the first time, the User ID file transfers to your computer and by default is placed in the \Notes\Data directory or folder. You want to be careful to protect this file, because someone else could use it to pretend to be you on the Lotus Notes network. If your computer operating system is password-protected, that might be enough. If your computer is accessible to several people, however, or if you share a computer at work, you might want to move the User ID file out of your computer onto a floppy disk for safekeeping. If you ever suspect the file is lost (along with your stolen laptop), report it to the Notes administrator.

LOCKING YOUR ID

After you've opened the Lotus Notes program and have been working with it, your personal information is at risk if you walk away from your desk and leave Lotus Notes running. You've already entered your password, so anyone who walks up to your desk can access any data that you can, including your mail database.

When you leave your desk, you should lock your ID so that no one else can access your Notes files without first entering your password. To lock your ID, choose **File**, **Tools**, **Lock ID** from the menu, or press **F5**, or click the **Lock ID** SmartIcon.

You can't always predict when you're going to be pulled away from your computer, and you might not have time to manually lock your ID. Notes can automatically lock your ID for you after a specified time period. To set up this automatic lock, choose **File**, **Tools**, **User Preferences** from the menu to open the User Preferences dialog box (see Figure 21.2). Enter the number of minutes in the Lock ID After____ Minutes of Inactivity field. Click **OK**.

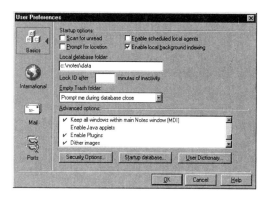

FIGURE 21.2   The User Preferences dialog box.

ACCESS CONTROL LIST

Lotus Notes has several features designed to limit access to documents, views, databases, and servers. For example, only authorized personnel can delete databases from the server, design applications, open certain documents, or read designated fields. The Notes administrator or the Application Designer controls most of this. What you are authorized to do depends on your status in the Access Control List of each database.

A database that contains all of your company's customers might be accessible to everyone in the company, but it's very possible that different people see different views, forms, and fields and can see only a partial list of customers. Perhaps each salesperson can see only the customers assigned to her when she opens the database, yet the sales manager sees all of the customers when he accesses the database.

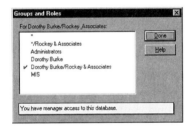 To determine your level of access for a particular database, click the database icon to select it; then, click the Access Key button on the status bar. The Groups and Roles dialog box appears, telling you what your access is (see Figure 21.3).

FIGURE 21.3 Groups and Roles dialog box.

Each person is granted one of seven levels of access to a database:

- **No Access**   This denies you access to the database. You can't read any of the documents in the database, and you can't create new documents. In fact, you cannot add the database icon to your workspace if you do not have access.

- **Depositor**   You can create documents but can't read any of the documents in the database—including the ones you create yourself. You might be granted this access level to cast a ballot in a voting database, for example.

- **Reader**   You can read the documents in the database, but you can't create or edit documents. You might have this level of access to a company policy database so that you can read policies but can't create or change them.

- **Author**   As an author, you can create documents and edit your own documents. You can't edit documents created by others, however, even though you can read them.

- **Editor**   You can do everything an author does, and you can edit documents submitted by others. A manager who approves the expense reports submitted by others needs at least editor access to those documents.

- **Designer**   A designer can do everything an editor can but also can create or change any design elements of the database. To change the design of a form in a database, you must have designer access.

- **Manager**   Can access everything a designer can. A manager also can assign and modify the Access Control List (ACL), modify replication settings, and delete a database from the server.

You probably will have at least reader access to the Public Address Book, whereas you have manager access to your Personal Address Book and Mail databases.

ENCRYPTION

When you want to keep your email private, encrypt it. Encrypting scrambles your message so that only the person receiving it can read it.

Each Lotus Notes user has unique *private* and *public* keys that Notes stores as part of the ID file. The public key is also stored in the person document for each user in the Public Address Book. When someone sends you an encrypted mail message, Notes uses your public key from the Public Address Book to encrypt the message. Now, no one but you can read it. At the delivery end, Notes uses your private key from your ID file to decrypt the message so that you can read it.

To encrypt a mail message, do the following:

1. Create the memo.

2. Click the **Delivery Options** button on the Action bar. The Delivery Options dialog box appears (see Figure 21.4).

FIGURE 21.4 The Delivery Options dialog box.

3. Check **Encrypt**.

4. Click **OK**.

To encrypt all the mail messages you send, do the following:

1. Choose **File**, **Tools**, **User Preferences**.

2. Click the **Mail** icon in the User Preferences dialog box.

3. Check **Encrypt Send Mail**.

4. Click **OK**.

If you want to decrypt all the mail that comes to you, do the following:

1. From the workspace, double-click the icon for your Public Address Book to open it.

2. Double-click the **People** folder to open it.

3. Open the document that shows your name (your person document).

4. Click the **Edit Person** button on the Action bar.

5. In the Encrypt Incoming Mail field near the bottom of the document, enter **Yes**.

6. Save and close the document.

7. Close the Public Address Book.

Can't Save Your Person Document?   If you can't save the document or you can't make the change, you'll have to ask your Notes administrator to do it for you. You might not have sufficient access to the Public Address Book to make modifications, not even to your own person document.

Encryption can be an important tool for laptop users. If you travel with Notes databases on your laptop, consult your Notes administrator about how to encrypt databases on your laptop and whether or not he recommends it.

SIGNATURES

A signature is an encoded and internal Notes function that prevents a user from masquerading as someone other than herself. To apply a signature to a message, the sender must have a Notes ID and know her password. For example, Jane, a Notes designer, can change her mail memo form to appear with Dorothy's name at the top and in the "from" field. She can send this message out, appearing to be Dorothy. Jane cannot *sign* the message as Dorothy, however, without knowing Dorothy's password and without having Dorothy's Notes ID. This is why you should protect your password and ID.

When a signature is applied in Notes, you see a message in the status bar that says "Signed by Jane Calabria." This assures you that Jane created this message (unless, of course, Jane was foolish enough to distribute her password and ID to someone else).

To sign a mail message, do the following:

1. Create a memo.

2. Click the **Delivery Options** button on the Action bar.

3. The Delivery Options dialog box appears (refer to Figure 21.4).

4. Check **Sign**.

5. Click **OK**.

If you want to add a signature to all your messages, do the following:

1. Choose **File**, **Tools**, **User Preferences**.

2. Click the **Mail** icon.

3. Check **Sign Sent Mail**.

4. Click **OK**.

In this lesson, you learned about Lotus Notes security and how to secure your own mail by using encryption and signatures. In the next lesson, you learn about replication.

UNDERSTANDING REPLICATION

22

In this lesson, you learn about replication, how to create a new Mail replica, and how to copy from the Public Address Book.

HOW REPLICATION WORKS

Notes servers store many databases. When you are in the office connected to the Notes network, you can open databases on the server directly from your workstation. Most of the databases that you access, including your mail database, are stored on your home server. You might be able to access databases on other Notes servers in your company, also.

Home Server The term used for the Domino server on which your mail database resides. You might find that you can access several Domino servers at work; the one containing your mail database is the one referred to as your "home" server.

When you are not in the office, however, you can access the server only by using a modem. If you have a lot of work to do in a database (such as reading and replying to mail), however, remaining on the phone line can be costly. Also, working via modem is much slower than being on the network in the office.

Lotus Notes enables you to read and reply to mail offline through *replication*, the process of "synchronizing" the same databases on different computers. It is actually a special type of copying process. Replication does not overwrite the entire database as copying the database does. Instead, it updates only the documents you modified, and it does the same thing for everyone who replicates the database. Then, as people call in and replicate a database, they receive the most recent copy of the documents in the database on their own computers. The server receives their changes, and the server sends them any updates that have occurred since they last replicated. Eventually, the modifications circulate to everyone using the database.

Here's an example of how replication works with regard to your Mail database. You call into the server and replicate your Mail database. After you've disconnected from the server, you read your mail and reply to some messages, delete some messages, and file some messages in folders. During this time, Mary Jones creates a new mail message for you, which is waiting on the server replica of your mail database. When you finish reading and replying to mail, you call into the server and replicate mail again. During this replication period, the changes you made while disconnected (new replies, deletions, and so forth) are sent to the server copy of your mail database, and Mary's new message is sent to your laptop replica of the database.

When you are ready to replicate a database, you place a telephone call from your computer (using your modem) to the server in your office. After the two computers "shake hands" and recognize each other, your computer begins sending updates you made to the database replicas. Then your computer receives any modifications made to the database since you last replicated. The replication process is illustrated in Figure 22.1.

Each database has a unique *replica ID* that identifies it as a genuine replica and not just a copy of the database (see Figure 22.2). If the database on your computer does not have the same ID as the one on the server, the server won't replicate the database.

Before replicating, the server also checks to see when the database on your computer was last modified. If that date is more recent than the date the database was last successfully replicated, then the database replicates. Lotus Notes maintains a replication history of each database you replicate (see Figure 22.3).

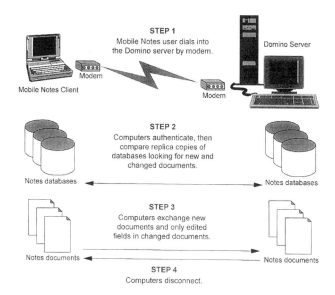

FIGURE 22.1   How replication works.

FIGURE 22.2   The Database Properties box displays the Replica ID.

FIGURE 22.3   The Replication History.

When the database replicates, it updates only those document fields that have been changed since the last replication and adds any new documents. Each document has its own *unique Notes identification number* assigned to it when it is first saved (see Figure 22.4). Part of that number is a document-level sequence number that increases each time you modify the document. If the number is higher for a particular document than the database on the server, it is replicated to the server.

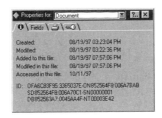

FIGURE 22.4   The Document Properties box displays the Unique Notes Identification number.

When replication is complete, hang up. You now have an updated copy of the database on your PC.

CREATING A NEW MAIL REPLICA

Before you can create a new replica, you need to set up for mobile use, as described in Lesson 23, "Working Remotely with Notes." Then, you create a new Mail replica. You need to call the server to do this. This step is only necessary if you don't see your mail database on your workspace. You also should talk to your Notes administrator and confirm that you need a new Mail replica.

CALLING THE SERVER

To place a call from your computer to the server, follow these steps:

1. Choose **File**, **Mobile**, **Call Server** from the menu. The Call Server dialog box appears (see Figure 22.5).

2. Pick the name of the server you want to call (if you have more than one).

FIGURE 22.5   The Call Server dialog box.

3. Click **Auto Dial**.

When you've finished your call, choose **File**, **Mobile**, **Hang Up**. When the dialog box appears with your modem port highlighted, click **Hang Up**.

If you call from a location that requires you to call an operator before placing an outside call, follow these steps:

1. Choose **File**, **Mobile**, **Call Server**.

2. Click **More Options**. The expanded Call Server dialog box appears.

3. Click **Manual Dial**.

4. When you see the Notes prompt, pick up the phone and call the operator.

5. After the operator connects you to the outside line, dial the phone number of your server.

6. When the connection is made, hang up the phone and click **OK**.

MAKING NEW REPLICAS

Making a new replica is a one-step process. Lesson 24, "Using the Replicator Page," shows you how to update this replica (or replicate) on an ongoing basis. It's very important to make a new replica of a database only once:

1. Choose **File**, **Replication**, **New Replica**; or click the **New Replica** SmartIcon. Make sure you don't have any database icons selected before you do this.

2. The Choose Database dialog box appears (see Figure 22.6).

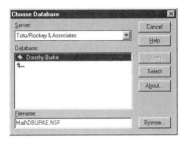

FIGURE 22.6   The Choose Database dialog box.

3. Under Server, choose your home server (if you are not currently connected, Lotus Notes prompts you to call the server).

4. From the Database list, select the file you want to replicate. Mail files are usually located in the \Mail subdirectory or folder, and your Mail file has your name on it.

5. Click **Select**.

6. In the New Replica dialog box (see Figure 22.7), make sure the Server displayed is **Local**. Notes automatically fills in the Title and the File Name.

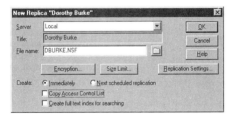

FIGURE 22.7   The New Replica dialog box.

7. Under Create, click **Immediately**.

8. Remove the check mark from **Copy Access Control List**.

9. Click **OK**.

After this, any time you want to replicate (update) your mail, use the Replicator page, as shown in Lesson 24.

PERSONAL ADDRESS BOOK

To send mail efficiently, you should keep your address books current. Before Notes sends your mail, it searches your Personal Address Book and then the Public Address Book. If you are working remotely, you need to populate your Personal Address Book with entries from the Public Address Book or replicate the Public Address Book to your laptop. If you work in a large company, the Public Address Book can take up quite a bit of hard-disk space on your laptop, so consider copying the addresses you need into your Personal Address Book.

To copy information from the Public Address Book, follow these steps:

1. While still online with your home server, choose **File**, **Database**, **Open**.

2. Under **Server**, select the name of your home server.

3. From the Database list, choose the name of your Public Address Book.

4. Click **Open**.

5. Open the **People** view.

6. Click the left margin next to the names of the person documents you want to copy. A check mark appears in front of each name to show it's selected.

7. Choose **Edit**, **Copy** or click the **Edit Copy** SmartIcon.

8. Press **Esc** to return to your workspace.

9. Open your Personal Address Book by double-clicking its icon and open the Business Cards view.

10. Choose **Edit**, **Paste** or click the **Edit Paste** SmartIcon.

In this lesson, you learned about replication, making a new Mail replica, and copying addresses from the Public Address Book to your Personal Address Book. In the next lesson, you will learn how Mail works for mobile users.

WORKING REMOTELY WITH NOTES

In this lesson, you learn how to
prepare and use Lotus Notes Mail remotely. You learn how to configure
your modem and location, as well as how to dial into the Lotus Notes
server. You also learn how to send and receive mail.

UNDERSTANDING MOBILE USERS

A *mobile* user is one who works in Notes while disconnected from the Notes network. You become a mobile user when you are working at a desktop computer from home or by using a laptop computer from a client site, a regional office, home, or hotel. As a mobile user, you can connect to the Notes network via a modem, instead of a LAN or WAN.

You do not want to read and reply to mail while connected to the server over a modem. Working while connected via a modem is time-consuming and possibly expensive, particularly if you are calling long distance. Therefore, mobile users generally replicate their mail databases to their laptops or desktops at home. You can work in your local replica, saving phone time for the replication process. You can access your data quickly, make and store all new documents and updates, and send everything back to the server in one short phone call.

To work remotely from home, a hotel room, or a location outside of the office in which you are not connected to your local area network, you need the following:

- A computer with Lotus Notes 4.6 or Notes Mail installed

- A modem connected to your PC

- A phone line for your modem

You also need the following information, which you can obtain from your Lotus Notes administrator:

- The name of your Lotus Notes server

- The phone number of the Lotus Notes server

- A copy of your certified Notes User ID (if you don't already have it)

With this information, you can configure your modem, create necessary Connection and Location documents and replicate mail, as described throughout this lesson.

WORKING WITH CONNECTION DOCUMENTS

To access a Domino server, you create a Server Connection document, which contains information about your server: the name of your server, the phone number to dial for your server, and the type of connection you are making (such as dial-in).

TIP   **Configuring Your Laptop**   Many companies have support people who can configure the laptop for you. But in some cases, you might have Lotus Notes Mail installed on your PC at home, or you might be a field person located far from the home office. In that situation, you need to perform the steps described in this lesson. Before you begin, ask your Lotus Notes administrator for the name of your Lotus Notes Mail server and the phone number to dial into the server.

To create a Server Connection document, follow these steps:

1. From your workspace, double-click your **Personal Address Book** database icon.

2. Select the **Advanced**, **Connections** view.

3. Click the **Add Connection** button on the Action bar.

4. The Server Connection document appears, as seen in
    Figure 23.1. Select the Connection Type as **Dialup
    Modem**.

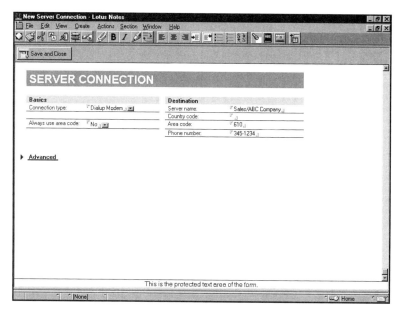

FIGURE 23.1   The Server Connection document.

5. Type the name of your mail database server in the Server
    Name field.

6. Fill in the Area Code and Phone Number fields.

7. If you must dial an area code to reach the server, change
    the Always Use Area Code field to **Yes**.

8. Under the Advanced section, select the port you'll be
    using by clicking the down arrow next to the **Modem
    port(s)** field. If you haven't enabled a port yet (see the
    next section on "Configuring Ports and Modems"), you
    can add the port later by editing the document.

9. Click the **Save and Close** button on the Action bar to
save this Server Connection document and close this
window.

If you are going to call into more than one server, you need a
Server Connection document for each. The exception is the use
of a *Passthru* server. You'll learn more about the Passthru server
in the "Creating Location Documents" section of this lesson.

CONFIGURING PORTS AND MODEMS

After you complete the server information in the Server Connection document, you need to specify a modem type and the port
your modem uses.

Ports   Computers have several "plugs" into which you
can plug cables or peripherals, which are called ports.
Each port has a name. When working remotely, ports
are called Com ports and are distinguished by number
(COM1, COM2 and so forth). Only one device, such as
your modem, can be assigned to each COM port.

1. Choose **File**, **Tools**, **User Preferences** from the menu.

2. In the User Preferences dialog box, click the **Ports** icon
(see Figure 23.2).

3. From the Communications Ports list, pick the port your
modem uses, such as COM1 or COM2.

4. Check **Port Enabled**.

5. Click the **Options** button (the name of the port is on the
button). The Additional Setup dialog box appears.

6. Specify the Modem Type you have (use the Autoconfigure
or generic all-speed modem type, if you don't know) and
enter any settings you need for your modem.

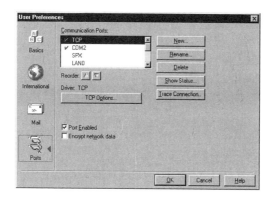

FIGURE 23.2   The User Preferences dialog box.

7. Click **OK** to exit the dialog box.

8. Click **OK** to exit User Preferences.

CREATING LOCATION DOCUMENTS

Notes always needs to know where you are when you are working, and the information it needs comes from a Location document. The Location document tells Notes details such as how to connect you to the network, where to find your mail database, how to dial the phone, and what port to use.

Five Location documents automatically appear during the installation process: Home (Modem), Office Network, Travel (Modem), Island (Disconnected), and Internet. You'll find them in your Personal Address Book in the Locations view. You can customize them to suit your needs or create your own Location documents.

Typically, the Ofice location is the one you use when you are in the office, connected to the LAN (Local Area Network) via a network port. Home is set up for a remote connection via modem, as is Travel. In the Travel Location document, however, you might want to specify your area code so that Notes dials 1 and the area code of your home server. The Home and Travel documents assume you are using a local replica of your mail database.

To customize the Home Location document, follow these instructions:

1. If the location indicated on the status bar is not "Home," click the location indicated on the status bar and choose **Home** as your location. "Home" is now your "current" location.

2. Click **Home** on the status bar and choose **Edit Current**. You'll see the Home Location document (see Figure 23.3).

TIP

Don't Want to Switch Location?   If you want to create a new Location document but don't want to switch your current location setting to do it, open your Personal Address Book, select the **Advanced**, **Locations** view, select the Location document you want to modify, and click the **Edit Location** button on the Action bar.

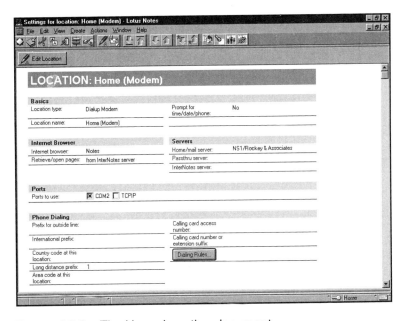

FIGURE 23.3   The Home Location document.

3. In the Basics section, choose **Dialup Modem**.

4. In the Servers section, enter the name of your home server in the Home/Mail Server field. Your home server is the server you connect to at work that stores your mail database. Type its full name (for example, Sales/ABC Company is the name of the server Sales in the organization ABC Company).

5. If you use a Passthru server, specify the name of that server in the Passthru Server field.

Passthru Server   Some companies have many Lotus Notes servers. They might determine that one of those servers will act as the traffic controller for incoming calls, referred to as a *Passthru* server because your call must pass through that server to reach the server where your mail is stored. Ask your Lotus Notes administrator if you're going to be dialing into a Passthru server. You need the Passthru server name and telephone number, as well as the server name that contains your mail database.

6. Complete the Phone Dialing section by providing your telephone dialing instructions.

7. In the Mail section complete the following:

   • **Mail File Location**   Choose **Local** to use a local replica of your Mail file or **On Server** if you connect directly to the server to use your mail.

   • **Mail File**   Enter the path and filename of your Mail file.

The remaining fields on this form contain either default information or don't apply to Mail options. Consult your Notes administrator if you're using an InterNotes server. Click the **Save and Close** button on the Action bar to save the file and close the document.

USING OUTGOING MAIL

When you installed Lotus Notes on your remote computer or laptop, you specified that you would be using a remote connection. As part of the installation process, Notes then created a replica *stub* (or place holder) of your mail database; the first time you attempt to open the database, Notes initializes the database by calling the server and making the full replica. If you have been using Notes from the office and only recently decided to go mobile, you have to make a replica of your mail database (as you did in Lesson 22, "Understanding Replication").

When working in a replica of the mail database, outoing mail is stored temporarily in the Outgoing Mailbox database. When you replicate or send mail to the server, the outgoing mail is sent, and the Outgoing Mailbox database mailbox is emptied.

 To see the mail that is waiting to be sent, double-click the Outgoing Mail icon on the workspace. You can view a list of the messages waiting delivery, but you can't read the mail message from the Outgoing Mail database.

> **TIP** **Getting Your Memo Back**   When you're connected to a LAN or WAN, you can't snatch your mail back after you've sent it. Deleting the Mail Memo from your mail database won't stop its delivery. When you work remotely, however, you can stop the mail before it gets to the server. If you haven't replicated or sent mail yet, the mail is still in the Outgoing Mail database. Open the database, select the mail message, and click the **Delete Message** button on the Action bar. You'll also have to delete your copy of it in your mail database.

REPLICATING MAIL

The Replicator page is the last page of your workspace. It provides a central location to handle all your replication needs. By using

WORKING REMOTELY WITH NOTES   197

the features available on the Replicator page, you can set options to control replication of your mail and any other databases you might use. Lotus Notes automatically creates a **Send Outgoing Mail entry** on the *Replicator* page, as shown in Figure 23.3. For information on how to configure your Replicator page, see Lesson 24, "Using the Replicator Page."

For each local database replica you have, you also see a database entry on the Replicator page. You can replicate these databases at the same time you replicate your mail. Click the check box (a check mark appears) at the beginning of the database entry row you want to include in the next replication.

In addition to your mail, your outgoing mail, and the database entries for all your replicated databases, the Replicator page has a call entry and a hangup entry that dial the server and hang up when replication is completed. All you have to do is click **Start**.

The status bar at the bottom of the page shows information about the current replication, letting you know when Lotus Notes is attempting to call a server, what database is being replicated, the progress of the replication, how many minutes are left, and when the replication finishes. After replication, the status bar displays statistics for individual entries.

USING SEND/RECEIVE MAIL

Before you leave the office to go on the road, make sure of the following:

- Your Location and Connection documents are set up.

- Your replicas are created, and you've added any necessary entries to the Replicator page.

- You have a phone cord, extra battery packs, and a power adapter.

- You have the phone number for your Notes administrator.

- You've loaded the Help Lite database, if you don't already have the Help database on your computer.

To send and receive mail while working remotely, follow these steps:

1. Plug one end of the phone cord into your modem's port and the other into a phone jack on the wall or on the back of a phone.

2. Make sure you disable call waiting on that line, or it will disconnect you from the server (try dialing *70).

3. Click the **Location** button on the status bar and choose your current location, if it's not already selected.

4. If you're not on the Replicator page, click the **Replicator** tab. Then choose one of the following methods:

   • Choose **Actions, Send and Receive Mail**.

   • Click the **Send & Receive Mail** button on the Action bar.

   • Choose **Actions, Send Outgoing Mail** (to send mail only).

Notes initializes the modem, and the call goes out to your server. Your new mail is replicated to the server, and the server replicates any new mail to your computer. After replication is complete, your computer hangs up. If you want to stop the mail from being sent or stop the replication process, click **Stop**. As soon as you return to the office, remember to switch your location back to one for connection to the network.

My Other Databases Didn't Replicate!   Sending and receiving mail does not replicate your other databases— only your mail database. You must click the **Start** button on the Replicator page to do that or click an individual database icon and choose **File, Replication, Replicate** from the menu.

MANAGING FILE SIZE

To keep your mail database at a manageable size, delete old mail frequently. On occasion, you should *compact* your databases to get rid of the empty spaces left by the deleted documents. You can compact any of the local replicas you have by doing the following:

1. Select the mail database icon on the workspace.

2. Choose **File**, **Database**, **Properties** from the menu or right-click the database icon and choose **Database Properties**.

3. When the Database Properties box appears, click the Information tab (see Figure 23.4).

4. Click the **% Used** button.

5. If the percentage is under 85 percent, click the **Compact** button. If not, you don't have to compact the database.

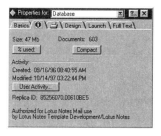

FIGURE 23.4   The Information page of the Database Properties box.

In this lesson, you learned how to work remotely with Notes. In the next lesson, you learn more about working with the Replicator page.

24 LESSON

USING THE REPLICATOR PAGE

In this lesson, you learn how to use the Replicator page and how to configure it by adding call, hangup, and database entries.

WHAT IS THE REPLICATOR PAGE?

The Replicator page is the last page of your workspace. It provides a central location to handle all your replication needs. By using the features available on the Replicator page (see Figure 24.1), you can set options to control which databases replicate, with which servers you are replicating, and whether you want to receive full or truncated (shortened) documents when you replicate.

There are several rows, or entries, on the Replicator page:

- **Start Replication at** Sets a schedule for replication. Most mobile users don't schedule their replications because that requires having the PC and Notes running during the scheduled time and configuring Notes to enable scheduled local agents to run.

- **Send outgoing mail** Sends all pending messages from your Outgoing Mail database.

  For each local database replica that you have, there is a database entry on the Replicator page.

- **Database templates** Templates are used to create new databases and to refresh the designs of any template-based databases you have. You probably will not need to replicate your templates with the server (you need to do this only to update your templates).

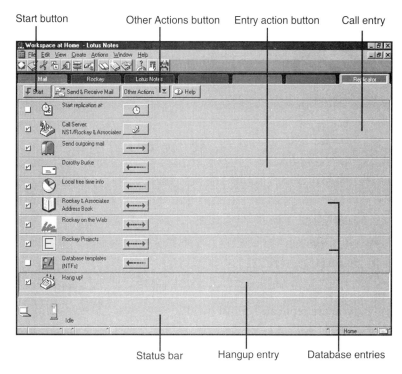

FIGURE 24.1   The Replicator page.

- **Call and hangup**   In addition to the automatic entry rows created for your databases, you can create call and hangup entries for automatic dialing from mobile locations to servers.

On each of the entry rows, there is an action button. Use these buttons to specify replication options relating to that entry row, such as whether to send or receive documents for that database; or, in the case of a call entry, use the button to specify the server and phone number to call.

Each entry row also has a check box. To include an entry in the replication, click the check box (a check mark appears). When you click the **Start** button on the Action bar, Lotus Notes performs the functions of each checked entry row in the order of the rows.

The status bar at the bottom of the page shows information about the current replication, letting you know when Lotus Notes is attempting to call a server, what database is being replicated, the progress of the replication, how many minutes are left, and when the replication is finished. After replication, the status bar displays statistics for individual entries.

CONFIGURING THE REPLICATOR PAGE

Except for a couple of the fixed entries on the Replicator page, you can move and delete entries to suit your needs.

To delete entries, do the following:

1. Click the entry you want to delete. This selects the entry.

2. Press the **Delete** key.

3. When asked if you want to delete the entry, select **Yes**.

 Be Careful when Deleting Database Entries! The settings for the databases on the Replicator page can be customized by location. If you remove a database from the Replicator page, however, it is removed for all locations. Instead of deleting the entry, remove the check mark to deselect it from the replication process.

Lotus Notes replicates the databases in the order they appear on the Replicator page. To move an entry, do the following:

1. Click the entry and hold down the mouse button.

2. Drag the entry to the position where you want it.

3. Release the mouse button.

The order of the databases and the databases that are checked for replication can be different for each location. From Home, you'll want the Outgoing Mail and your mail database high on the list.

From the Office location, you don't need to replicate your mail until you're ready to take your computer out of the office, so your mail database might not be checked for replication. To set up the page differently for each location, select the location first by clicking the **Location** button on the status bar and then rearrange the entries and check the ones you need at that location.

MAKING CALL AND HANGUP ENTRIES

If you are a mobile user, you will want to create call entries so that you can automatically connect to servers via modem, if Notes hasn't automatically created them for you (check your location because these entries don't usually appear for Office but do appear for Home). To create a call entry, do the following:

1. Using the Location button on the status bar, select a location in which you need to use a modem to connect to the server. Home or Travel are possible settings.

2. Click the entry that you want to appear immediately below your call entry.

3. Choose **Create**, **Call Entry**.

    (**Optional**) By default, the call entry specifies your home server. To specify a different server, double-click the call entry action button; select the server you want to call, and then click **OK**. The list of servers that appears only includes those servers that have specified telephone numbers. If you need to add another server to the list or have to change a telephone number, choose **File**, **Mobile**, **Server Phone Numbers**.

After your replication tasks are complete, you need to disconnect the modem from the telephone line. A hangup entry does this automatically for you.

To create a hangup entry, do the following:

1. Using the Location button on the status bar, select a location in which you need to use a modem to connect to the server.

2. Click the entry you want to appear immediately below the hangup entry (you can always move the entry if you get it in the wrong place).

3. Choose **Create**, **Hangup Entry**.

Even if you have more than one call entry, you only need one hangup entry. The Replicator hangs up automatically from the first call entry when it encounters a new call entry, so you only need to hang up after the final call.

USING SELECTIVE REPLICATION

When you are working remotely, it helps to replicate only a portion of your mail database to reduce the time allotted for replication and save on telephone charges.

One method for doing this is to replicate only a portion of each mail message so that you receive only the essential part when you're working remotely:

1. Click the database entry action button for your mail. The Replication dialog box appears, as shown in Figure 24.2.

FIGURE 24.2   The Replication dialog box.

2. Under Replicate with Server, choose **Any Available**, **Try Last Successful First**.

3. Select in which direction you want to replicate by checking **Send Documents to Server** and/or **Receive Documents from Server**.

4. When you choose to receive documents from the server, select one of the options from the list box: **Receive Full Documents**, **Receive Summary and 40K of Rich Text Only** (long memos and attachments are cut short), or **Receive Summary Only**. The summary includes only basic information, such as the author and subject.

5. Click **OK**.

If you choose to receive less than the full document, it doesn't mean you can't get the whole document later. When you need the remainder of the document, do the following:

1. Open the document for which you need the complete text, or select several documents.

2. Choose **Actions**, **Retrieve Entire Document**.

3. Select **Get Documents Now Via BackGround**.

4. Click **OK**.

Many of the options you have for replicating databases are in the Replication Settings dialog box (see Figure 24.3), which you can access by clicking the database entry with the right mouse button and then selecting **Replication Settings** from the menu.

Figure 24.3   Replication Settings dialog box.

Use the following settings to limit what you replicate in the selected database:

- With the **Space Savers** icon selected, check **Remove Documents Not Modified in the Last** and specify the number of days. This purges old documents from your replica.

- To receive only selected folders and views, check **Replicate a Subset of Documents**. Then, select one or more folders and views that you need.

- To receive only selected documents, check **Replicate a Subset of Documents**. Check **Select by Formula**. Enter the formula. Do not attempt this if you are unfamiliar with Lotus Notes formulas.

- Click the **Send** icon and check **Do Not Send Deletions Made in This Replica to Other Replicas** so you don't replicate documents you have deleted from the replica since the replica's last purge interval. This leaves the mail database on the server intact.

- With the **Other** icon selected, enter a cutoff date in the box below **Only Replicate Incoming Documents Saved or Modified After**. This guarantees that you will only receive recent documents, and it doesn't purge old documents from the database.

- Also on the Advanced page (see Figure 24.4), check **Deletions** to remove any documents from your replica that already have been deleted from the source database.

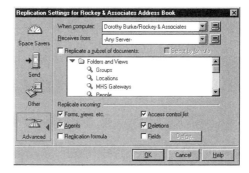

FIGURE 24.4   Replication Settings dialog box with Advanced selected.

In this lesson, you learned how to configure the Replicator page and how to use selective replication. In the next lesson, you will learn how to use Notes to send and receive Internet mail.

25 SENDING MAIL VIA THE INTERNET

In this lesson, you learn about creating, receiving, and sending mail via the Internet and Lotus Notes.

INTERNET MAIL WITH THE NOTES SERVER

When you want to send mail to non-Notes Mail users or Notes users in other domains via the Internet, you should start by consulting your Notes administrator. Your Notes administrator can tell you how your company's Notes network is set up to handle Internet mail.

When the Notes server has an Internet connection, sending and receiving mail via the Internet is similar to sending and receiving any Notes mail messages.

For example, you can add Business Cards to your Personal Address Book that list Internet email addresses, and you can enter a person with an Internet address as one of the recipients of a mail message the same way you would anyone else. For a single message, you must enter the full Internet address (such as **dburke@ planetnotes.com**) instead of the person's name in the To, cc, or bcc field of your mail message.

Be aware that any Notes message sent via the Internet probably will lose most of its formatting, any graphics or tables, any embedded objects, and possibly its attachments. Messages sent through the Internet are converted to plain text, and the formatting is removed. If you know you're sending your message through the Internet to another Notes user, however, you might be able to preserve some of the Notes formatting. While you're creating the message, choose **Actions**, **Special Options** from the menu. Select **I Am Sending This Notes Document to Other Notes Mail User(s) Through the Internet**. Click **OK**.

If you're sending mail to a non-Notes user and he complains that your attachments are garbled or don't arrive at all, ask your recipient if his mail system uses the MIME (Base 64) encoding system. He'll have to get back to you on that. When he does, be sure he finds out what encoding system he has, so you can select a different method of encoding attachments. Then, when you send him another message with an attachment, choose **Actions**, **Special Options** from the menu. Select his encoding method from the Encoding Method for Internet Mail Attachments field and click **OK**.

INTERNET MAIL WITHOUT THE NOTES SERVER

Your company might not be set up to send Internet mail from the Notes server, but if you can have a personal mail account on the Internet you can set up Notes to send Internet mail from your own PC. The mail system you use must support POP3 Internet protocol (your Internet service provider should be able to tell you that) to send and receive mail with Notes.

To set up your Internet mail through Notes, you have to do two things: Create a database for your Internet mail and create a Location document that contains information about your Internet mail system.

CREATING A DATABASE FOR YOUR INTERNET MAIL

Users who are connected on a LAN (local area network) or WAN (wide area network) don't normally keep a copy of their mail databases on their own PCs. To use Internet mail from your PC, you must have a mail database there to store your Internet mail. You can either create a new Internet mail database or create a new replica of your existing mail database (useful if you want to see both types of mail in one database).

If you're a mobile user, you already have a replica of your mail database on your computer. You can use that replica for Internet mail, as well. You should check with your Notes Administrator, however, to be sure that your mail database on the server and the replica on your PC have both been updated to use the Release 4.6 mail database design.

To create a new mail database on your computer for Internet mail, follow these steps:

1. Choose **File**, **Database**, **New** from the menu.

2. In the New Database dialog box (see Figure 25.1), select **Local** as the Server.

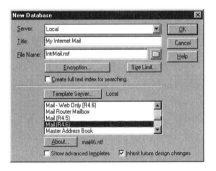

Figure 25.1 The New Database dialog box.

3. Enter a title for the database (such as "My Internet Mail") in the Title field. This is the title that appears on the database icon.

4. In the File Name box, enter the filename of the database (such as "IntrMail.nsf").

5. From the list of templates, choose **Mail (R4.6)**.

6. Click **OK**.

To create a replica of your mail database so that you can store Internet and Notes messages in the same database, follow these steps:

1. Check with your Notes Administrator to make sure that your mail database has been upgraded with the Release 4.6 mail database design.

2. From the workspace, select your mail database icon.

3. Choose **File**, **Replication**, **New Replica** from the menu or click the **New Replica** SmartIcon. The New Replica dialog box appears (see Figure 25.2).

FIGURE 25.2   The New Replica dialog box.

4. From the Server list, select **Local**.

5. The Title of the database is entered for you, but you can change the File Name, if you choose to.

6. Click **OK**.

For more detailed information on replication and creating a new mail replica, see Lesson 22.

CREATING A LOCATION DOCUMENT FOR YOUR INTERNET MAIL

To store the details of your Internet mail system for Notes, you must create a new Location document or modify an existing one. For more information on Location documents, see Lesson 23.

To create or modify a location document, do the following:

1. Open your Personal Address Book.

2. From the navigator pane, select the **Advanced**, **Locations** view.

3. To create a new location document, click the **Add Location** button on the Action bar. To modify an existing document, select the document (such as **Internet**) and click the **Edit Location** button on the Action bar. The Internet location document is shown in Figure 25.3.

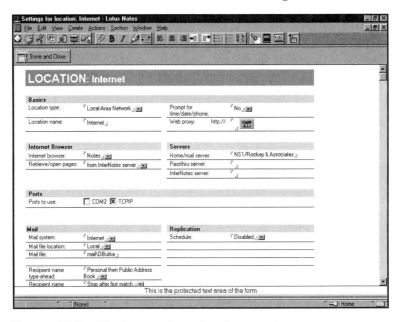

FIGURE 25.3   The Internet Location document.

4. Under the Basics section, select a **Location Type** by clicking the down arrow next to the field. Select **Local Area Network** if you will be connected to your Internet mail system when you create and send mail. If you won't be connected but will store the mail and send it later, select **No Connection**.

To Be Connected or Not Be Connected?   If you're not always going to be connected when you're creating mail, create two location documents—one for each situation.

TIP

5. Enter a name for the location in the Location Name field.

6. Under the Ports section, select **TCPIP** in the Ports to Use field.

TCP/IP Isn't a Choice!   To enable the TCP/IP port, choose **File**, **Tools**, **User Preferences**. Click the **Ports** icon. Select **TCPIP** from the Communications Port list. Select **Port Enabled**. Click **OK**. *Note*: You must have TCP/IP enabled in your operating system also (ask your Notes or System Administrator for help).

TIP

7. Under the Mail section (see Figure 25.4), select **Internet** as the Mail System. Your Mail File Location is Local.

8. In the Mail File field, enter the name of the database file you created or the filename of the replica.

9. Under the Internet Mail section, type your Internet email address (the address people use to send you mail over the Internet) in the Internet Mail Address field.

10. In the Outgoing (SMTP) Internet Mail field, enter the name of your outgoing mail server (available from your Internet service provider).

11. Type the name of your incoming mail server (ask your Internet Service Provider) in the Incoming Internet Mail Server field.

12. Enter the name of your Internet mail account in the Internet Username field. This is also available from your ISP (Internet service provider).

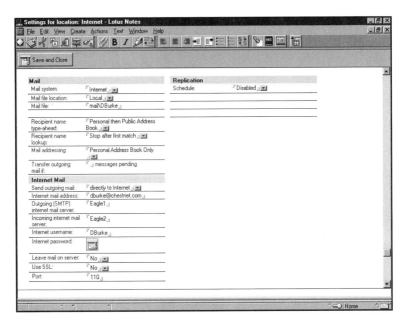

FIGURE 25.4   The Mail and Internet Mail sections of the Location document.

13. Enter the password you use to access your Internet mail in the Internet Password field.

14. Click **Save** and **Close**.

You are now ready to create and send mail.

CREATING INTERNET MAIL

Creating mail for the Internet is very similar to creating Notes mail. However, you won't be able to use Notes Mail delivery options, letterhead, mail encryption, mail signatures, or workflow features (meeting invitations, tasks, or serial route memos).

To create Internet mail, do the following:

1. Choose the Location document for the Internet by clicking the **Location** button on the status bar and selecting

the name of your Internet Location document. If you
have two locations (connected and disconnected), select
the one that's appropriate.

2. Create a mail memo the same way you would a Notes
   mail message, except that when you enter To, cc, and bcc
   information you must use addresses that conform to
   Internet needs (such as **dburke@planetnotes.com**).

3. Send the message.

SENDING AND RECEIVING INTERNET MAIL

Mail transfers immediately to your Internet mail system when
you click the **Send** button, if you're connected. If you're disconnected when you create a mail message, it gets stored in the Outgoing Mail database when you click **Send**.

To send the messages stored in your Outgoing Mail database,
select the appropriate Location document and then do one of the
following:

- From the status bar, click the **Mail** icon and select Send
  Outgoing Mail from the pop-up menu (select Send and
  Receive Mail to do both at the same time).

- From the Replicator Page, click the **Send and Receive
  Mail** button to do both at the same time. Or, to just send
  mail, check the box next to the **Send Outgoing Mail**
  entry, remove any checks from database entries, and click
  Start.

To receive Internet mail, make sure you have the appropriate location document selected and then do one of the following:

- From the status bar, click the Mail icon and select Receive
  Mail.

- From the Replicator page, check the box for the entry of
  the mail database you created, remove any checks in
  boxes for other database entries, and click **Start**.

Open the mail database you created to check your mail.

In this lesson, you learned about sending Internet mail via your Notes server or setting up your own computer for using Notes with your Internet mail system.

INDEX

launching, 116
printing, 117
viewing, 113-115
deleting, 101-102
from folders, 105
delivery options, 81-82
Mood Stamps, 84-85
priority, 83
reports, 83-84
folders, 102-105
forwarding, 100
links, 119-120
anchor, 123-124
database, 124-125
document, 120-123
opening, 88-89
printing, 94-95
read marks, 89-91
replying to, 96-100
saving copies, 87
sections, 63-65
send options, 85-86
tables, 66-67
formatting, 68, 71
rows and columns, 67-68
views, 91-92
Discussion Thread,
105-106
Preview pane, 92-94
encrypting mail messages,
81-82, 177-179
Event entry, Calendar, 155
expanded Index view, 34-35
expanded sections, 64-65

F

F1 (Help) key, 33
Favorite Topics view, 36
Favorites database, 165
Favorites portfolio
databases
adding, 167-169
deleting, 169-170
navigating, 166-167

fields, security, Access Control
List, 4-5, 172, 175-177
file attachments, 111
creating, 111-113
detaching, 115-116
launching, 116
printing, 117
viewing, 113-115
file compression, 112
File Print dialog box, 94-95,
117, 163-164
finding Help information,
37-39
floating palette, 20
folders
email messages, 102-105
mail databases, 26-28
font sizes, workspace pages,
13-14
fonts, 56
formatting
tables, 68, 71
text, 53-56
color, 56-57
paragraphs, 57-62
forms, 4-5
forwarding email messages,
100
Free Time dialog box, 160-161

G-H

groups, 78-80
Groups and Roles dialog box,
176
Guide Me searches (Help),
37-39
Guide Me SmartIcon, 33

handup entries, 203-204
Help, 31-33
menu, 34-36
Notes Mobile Survival Kit,
40
searches, 37-39

Notes Client, 2
servers, Internet mail,
208-209
unique Notes identification
number, 184
Notes Mobile Survival Kit, 40
numbered or bulleted lists, 60

O

Open Database dialog box, 169
opening
email messages, 88-89
mail databases, 22
Options dialog box, 163
Out of Office message re-
sponse, 132, 135
Outgoing Mail database,
196-197

P

pages
database icons, moving to
other pages, 11
tabs
adding to workspace, 11
colors, 9-10
naming, 9-10
palettes, floating, 20
panes
mail database windows,
22-23
resizing, 24
Preview, 92-94
paragraphs
aligning, 57-58
bulleted or numbers lists, 60
indenting, 59
setting tabs, 60-62
spacing, 60
Passthru servers, 195
passwords, 172-174

pentagons, indent, 59
Permanent Pen SmartIcon, 57
permanent pens (color), 57
Personal Address Book,
45, 72-74
Business Cards, 75-77
copying from Public, 187
creating messages, 80
groups, 78-80
location document for
Internet mail, 212
Personal Stationery template,
128-130
phone messages, 136
pop-up text, 125-126
portfolios
Favorites
adding databases,
167-169
deleting databases,
169-170
navigating, 166-167
rearranging databases,
170-171
templates, 165
ports, configuring for mobile
users, 192-193
Prevent Copying option
(Delivery Options dialog
box), 84
Preview pane, 92-94
Print SmartIcon, 94
Printed Books view, 36
printing
Calendar, 163-164
email messages, 94-95
file attachments, 117
private key, 177
properties, workspace, 9-11
Properties box, 15-17
Properties SmartIcon, 55
Public Address Book, 45,
72-73, 187
public key, 177

Need more information on Lotus Notes and Domino 4.6? Check out these other titles from Macmillan Computer Publishing...

10 Minute Guide to Lotus Notes 4.6

ISBN: 0-7897-1536-8 $14.99 USA/$21.95 CDN   224 pages

Build upon the knowledge of *10 Minute Guide to Lotus Notes Mail 4.6* with this book focused on the Notes 4.6 desktop client. The *10 Minute Guide to Lotus Notes 4.6* offers simple, practical help for busy people who need fast results. Learn to configure calendaring and scheduling options, use the new Notes 4.6 Favorites database, participate in discussion databases, and search the Web, all using the consumer-tested *10 Minute Guide* format. This book is the perfect addition to your Notes 4.6 desktop reference collection.

Teach Yourself Lotus Notes 4.6 in 24 Hours

ISBN: 0-672-31256-5 $19.99 USA/$28.95 CDN   400 pages

For a broader look of Notes' more advanced features, check out *Teach Yourself Lotus Notes 4.6 in 24 Hours*. With this easy-to-use tutorial, you'll learn to customize your workspace, use tables and sections within documents, work with web browsers, work remotely using Notes, and much more. You'll find all you need to get up-to-speed with Notes 4.6—and be able to do it in only 24 Hours!

Special Edition Using Lotus Notes and Domino 4.6

ISBN: 0-7897-1535-X $49.99 USA/$70.95 CDN   1050 pages/1 CD-ROM

For a more in-depth look into the Notes and Domino environment, check out *Special Edition Using Lotus Notes and Domino 4.6*. This book focuses on the features and tools that help you to accomplish your tasks in the most efficient manner. You'll find support for the latest Internet protocols and the administration enhancements included in Version 4.6. Expert authors provide comprehensive, in-depth analysis of Lotus Notes and Domino 4.6 for you to go beyond the basics of groupware. You'll find the entire book on the CD-ROM in Notes database format, as well as software from several vendors that will help you get your Notes network running optimally in no time at all.

To order one or more of these titles, call 1-800-428-5331 or visit www.mcp.com